PENGUIN BOOKS

Mortal Syntax

June Casagrande is a writer and journalist whose weekly column, "A Word, Please," appears in several community news supplements to the *Los Angeles Times* and in papers in Texas and Florida. She has written articles for a number of regional and national publications, and has worked as an editor and copy editor. Casagrande was born in New York City, grew up in the Clearwater/St. Petersburg/Tampa area, and now lives in Pasadena, California. *Mortal Syntax* is her second book.

For more information, visit www.grammarsnobs.com.

Mortal Syntax

101 Language Choices That Will
Get You Clobbered by the Grammar Snobs
—Even If You're Right

JUNE CASAGRANDE

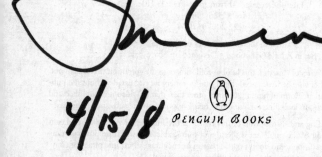

4/15/8

PENGUIN BOOKS

PENGUIN BOOKS
Published by the Penguin Group
Penguin Group (USA) Inc., 375 Hudson Street, New York, New York 10014, U.S.A.
Penguin Group (Canada), 90 Eglinton Avenue East, Suite 700,
Toronto, Ontario, Canada M4P 2Y3 (a division of Pearson Penguin Canada Inc.)
Penguin Books Ltd, 80 Strand, London WC2R 0RL, England
Penguin Ireland, 25 St Stephen's Green, Dublin 2,
Ireland (a division of Penguin Books Ltd)
Penguin Group (Australia), 250 Camberwell Road, Camberwell,
Victoria 3124, Australia (a division of Pearson Australia Group Pty Ltd)
Penguin Books India Pvt Ltd, 11 Community Centre,
Panchsheel Park, New Delhi–110017, India
Penguin Group (NZ), 67 Apollo Drive, Rosedale, North Shore 0632,
New Zealand (a division of Pearson New Zealand Ltd)
Penguin Books (South Africa) (Pty) Ltd, 24 Sturdee Avenue,
Rosebank, Johannesburg 2196, South Africa

Penguin Books Ltd, Registered Offices:
80 Strand, London WC2R 0RL, England

First publishd in Penguin Books 2008

1 3 5 7 9 10 8 6 4 2

Copyright © June Casagrande, 2008
All rights reserved

LIBRARY OF CONGRESS CATALOGING IN PUBLICATION DATA
Casagrande, June.
Mortal syntax : 101 language choices that will get you clobbered by
the grammar snobs—even if you're right / June Casagrande.
p. cm.
ISBN 978-0-14-311332-4
1. English language—Usage. 2. English language—Syntax.
3. English language—Errors in usage. 1. Title.
PE1460.C326 2007
425—dc22 2007012074

Printed in the United States of America
Set in Adobe Garamond • Designed by Elke Sigal

Except in the United States of America, this book is sold subject to the condition that it shall not, by way of trade or otherwise, be lent, resold, hired out, or otherwise circulated without the publisher's prior consent in any form of binding or cover other than that in which it is published and without a similar condition including this condition being imposed on the subsequent purchaser.

The scanning, uploading and distribution of this book via the Internet or via any other means without the permission of the publisher is illegal and punishable by law. Please purchase only authorized electronic editions, and do not participate in or encourage electronic piracy of copyrighted materials. Your support of the author's rights is appreciated.

For Donna Stallings

. . .

American English remains vibrant and effective precisely because we're skeptical of authorities.

—DENNIS BARON

It is a virtue to attend to what others are trying to say, instead of seizing gleefully on their inadvertences and shrieking, "Gotcha!"

—BARBARA WALLRAFF

Beware of the man who works hard to learn something, learns it, and finds himself no wiser than before.

—KURT VONNEGUT

Contents

PART IV *Noun Sequitur*

Introduction

The Princess and the Peeved:
A Fairly Telling Fairy Tale

*O*nce upon a time, a beautiful princess began writing a grammar column.

The column was titled "A Word, Please." It was not titled "Every Curmudgeon's Long-Awaited Opportunity to Rant Like a Lunatic About Other People's Grammar Mistakes." It was not titled "A Public Address to the Mentally Unstable as They Prepare to Set Out on Punctuation-Related Killing Sprees." And it surely was not titled "Please Find Errors in This Column, Then Write to Tell Me You're Smarter Than Me."

Yet rant they did. Find errors they did. Write to her about them they did (and will again as soon as they see that she wrote "smarter than me" instead of "smarter than I"—an issue covered quite regally in chapter 57 of this book).

And their e-mails inspired a book. And the book was titled *Grammar Snobs Are Great Big Meanies.* It was not titled *Everyone Who Has Ever Corrected Anyone Else's Grammar Must Therefore Be a Snob.* It was not titled *Be Ashamed That You Know How to Use "Whom."* And it certainly was not titled *Please Find Errors in This Book and Publish Them in Your Snooty Boston Globe Column.*

Yet worry some did. Misinterpret some did. Publicly de-pants our beautiful princess some did.

So our princess realized she had more work to do.

First, she realized that people still had many more questions about grammar snobbery. Some wanted to know, "Does wincing when I hear *nuclear* pronounced *nu-cu-lar* make me a grammar snob?" Others wanted to know, "Seriously, what's wrong with those psychos who jump on me for saying *a myriad of* before they even open their dictionaries to make sure they're right?" (The answers to these questions are "no" and "adult diaper rash," respectively.)

The second thing our beautiful princess realized is that she must scour all her old e-mails, all her grammar books, and even the Internet to compile a list of the language issues creating the most confusion for nice people and thereby creating fodder for the grammar snobs.

And finally, she realized she must write another book compiling 101 of these most commonly attacked usages—a book with lots more errors in it to keep certain smug columnists and other humorless types chained to their keyboards and thus off the streets.

This is that book.

Each short chapter is dedicated to a single language issue—in the form of a single sentence—that can incite a grammar snob to verbal violence.

Indeed, most of these issues our princess culled from her brushes with and study of real-life grammar snobs—be they readers of her column, authors of books, or denizens of that bottomless reservoir of grammar griping: the Internet. And in braving this frightening terrain, our princess confirmed a horrifying truth: that her subjects' syntax need not be mistaken to be chided. Indeed, oftentimes when some poor speaker or writer is being attacked, it is the attacker—not the attackee—who is wrong. Which leads us to the single most important truth about grammar snobs: Though they claim to be champions of the language, in truth many care more about criticizing others than about getting their facts straight.

Thus, each chapter has at its beginning an at-a-glance reference: "This Usage Is . . ." Here our princess explains whether the construction in question is "right," "wrong," "so wrong," "not cut-and-dried," "embarrassing," "very unwise," "risky," "rock solid," etc. These chapter toppers will allow readers to see whether a usage is acceptable without having to first wade through long stories about the princess's cats and her frequent Vegas junkets.

It is important to note that the opinions she offers here are not her own (barring the occasional jab at certain wicked witches of the grammar world and Fox News). Our lovely princess has no desire to make the rules. There are enough jesters doing that already. Our princess instead has based each ruling on the consensus of her merry court of fourteen advisors. They are: *The Chicago Manual of Style; The Associated Press Stylebook; Garner's Modern American Usage; Fowler's Modern English Usage;* Strunk and White's *The Elements of Style; The Oxford English Grammar; Webster's New World College Dictionary; The American Heritage Dictionary of the English Language,* Fourth Edition; *Lapsing into a Comma; The Elephants of Style; The Careful Writer; Usage and Abusage;* Barbara Wallraff's *Word Court;* and *The Dictionary of Disagreeable English.*

The insights of these royal advisors are at times supplemented from other sources, including the columns of James J. Kilpatrick, the book *Far from the Madding Gerund* and the blog that spawned it, and *The Complete Idiot's Guide to Grammar and Style.*

More on all these sources is available in the section royally dubbed Sources.

Our princess is aware that there exist other texts that are just as worthy of inclusion. She does not care. Indeed, for any resulting oversight she blames all of her royal subjects who failed to purchase copies of *Grammar Snobs.* Had more done so, they could have afforded our princess the means to purchase and consider every language book under the sun, including her very own copy of the $900 *Oxford English Dictionary*, as well as the services of royal apprentices to peruse them between cappuccino runs and foot rubs.

In consulting these wise men and women, our princess observed the following philosophy: None of them reigns supreme. If one sage advisor says that a usage is permissible—for example, that it's okay to use "fun" as an adjective—and others say it's not permissible, followers can choose whichever authority they like. Thus, anyone who wishes to use it so has on his side an authority to sanction his choice. And therefore, it is permissible.

Indeed, our princess's aim is not to tell people how they *should* use the language. She seeks only to help people know how they *can* use the language, if they so choose, with the full blessings of these most regal advisors.

It's of no little import that some of said advisors are grammar books, others are style guides, and still others are usage guides. Grammar books such as *The Oxford English Grammar* attempt to describe the mysterious mechanical workings of the language, but style books like *The Chicago Manual of Style* and *The Associated Press Stylebook* have a different task. Their job is to offer guidance to specific groups of writers and, at times, make difficult calls for consistency's sake. Thus, their advice is not necessarily right or wrong but the best possible guidance they can offer to their users. Usage guides such as *Fowler's Modern English Usage* and *Garner's Modern American Usage* take a somewhat similar approach but they take it to a much broader audience—all those who want to know which choices are widely considered "good English."

Again, our princess does not play favorites with these authorities. She merely researches their wisdom and conveys the options these experts leave open to you.

So, with courage in her heart and a few of her own meanie detractors in her sights, the beautiful princess wrote her oh-so-important book, dreaming it would one day lift the curse of grammar snobbery from the land. Her great hope was that, far and wide, everyone would learn that "went missing" is a perfectly acceptable term that cannot rightly incur a snob's criticism. That they would find out that "I feel bad" is the correct choice over "I feel badly," except when talking about ill-fated prom dates. That they would discover that "myself" is not an object pronoun and therefore should not be used to replace "me." And that they would see that incomplete sentences can sometimes be used to brilliant effect. And sometimes not.

But most of all, the princess dreamed that someday everyone—normal people and recovering grammar snobs—would learn how to live happily ever after, free from the evil curse she has dubbed "mortal syntax," until the end of their many peaceful and prosperous days.

PART I

The Biggies

*(If you learn just seventeen things about language
before losing interest in the subject altogether, make it these!)*

1

I feel <u>bad</u>.

This usage is: Correct (yes, really).

*W*hen I was a child, one of the major pudding manufacturers introduced something called the Pudding Shaker. I don't recall which brand, but I'm sure it was among the pudding industry's Big Ten—a group that includes Jell-O, Jell-O, Jell-O, and Pud-4-Less.

The Pudding Shaker consisted of a large plastic tumbler with a lid and was designed to free the masses from the exhausting, soul-crushing process of making instant pudding with an electric mixer. You just put your instant pudding powder and some milk into the shaker, close the lid, and shake. And voilà. In no time—delicious, rich, creamy pudding. Or at least that's how it worked in the commercial. The real-life results looked more like clumpy, runny brown milk spattered on the floor and walls (a mess easily blamed on any geriatric dog). But based on what I saw in the commercials, a bad outcome could only be the result of user error.

As you may have inferred from my story, there was a Pudding Shaker in my home. Which means that someone in my home bought one. Which means that we were a family of idiots.

But we weren't complete, hopeless idiots because, unlike hopeless types, we had the capacity to learn. By the time one of the major pasta sauce companies introduced "the sauce you toss"—a marinara distinct from any other on the market in that it was specially formulated to be mixed in with your spaghetti *before* you put it on the plate—I had finally gotten wise. I managed to resist the urge to purchase this product, despite its promise to solve all my vexing pasta problems. Around the same time, I was also able to resist the McDLT—the hamburger that kept the patty separate from the vegetables until you were ready to eat. By then I was wise, jaded even. And I'd grown all but immune to the threat of hot lettuce.

As you're about to see, some chapter lead-ins in this book are transparent and shameless attempts to lure you into reading about grammar and usage. Other chapters are more succinct and direct, suggesting the possibility that I had more important things on my mind, such as the Thursday night *My Name Is Earl* and *The Office* lineup or perhaps the demanding task of curling up into the fetal position and sobbing, "I can't come up with anything clever. I'm all washed up!"

But this pudding business has a direct correlation. It is this: I'm sick of being jerked around. And when it comes to copular verbs, also called linking verbs, a lot of us have been seriously jerked around.

Most of us were taught that adverbs modify verbs. But an alarmingly small proportion of us learned about copular or linking verbs, which can seem to turn our basic understanding of adverbs on its head. So we have no choice but to assume that "I feel badly" is the correct choice over "I feel bad."

Unfortunately, that just isn't so.

To understand the principle of copular or linking verbs, ask yourself: Why do you say "I am happy" instead of "I am happily"? It's because "happy" is really describing the subject "I" and not the action of the verb, right? That's a good place to begin understanding copular verbs, but it doesn't end there.

The most common copular verb is "to be." Many others also refer to states of being or to senses: "seem," "appear," "act," "become," "look," "remain," "get," "grow," "smell," "feel," "taste."

And the rule we've been accidentally yet so conveniently kept in the dark about is this: Copular verbs take *adjectives* as their complements, not adverbs:

> The dog appears hungry (not hungrily).
> The suspect acts guilty (not guiltily).
> The haggis smells bad (not badly).
> John became angry (not angrily).

Of course, most copular verbs aren't exclusively copular. The word "appears" in the above example describes the dog, so it's copular and takes an adjective. But if you wanted to say that the dog "appears suddenly," it's not copular because you're describing an action—appearing. Another example: "Feel" is copular when describing a mental state, but when you're describing the action of touching and feeling, it's not copular. That's why "I feel badly" isn't always wrong. On the contrary, it could be spot-on when discussing a bad Braille reader or a clumsy prom date. But it's not the right choice if you're a former ad exec repenting for your past sins. So if you're the person who came up with the Pudding Shaker or a manipulative slogan like "Mayonnaise: The Other White Meat," you should feel bad. Very, very bad.

2

I feel <u>good</u>.

This usage is: Perfectly acceptable.

*A*s you may have noticed, there are a lot of organizations out there that want you to believe they're listening to you. There are those AOL "click here to register your opinion" surveys, usually about critical matters such as whether Nicole Richie was wrong to speak while drunk or whether Mel Gibson was wrong to speak while drunk or whether Burt Reynolds's plastic surgeon was wrong to operate while drunk. There are the Fox News invitations to vote, via text message, on just how super the last presidential speech was. And there are those incredibly transparent questions like "How do you feel about that?" put forth by your unconvincingly attentive spouse.

After a while, it becomes clear to all but the most vote-happy web surfer that these people and organizations don't really want to hear our opinions. They just know how to exploit an ugly fact of modern existence: We're all desperate to have our voices heard. In our age of one-way mass communication addiction, we all just want someone to listen to us.

Little do we know that some people out there *are* listening. In fact, they're hanging on our every word. But not in a good way. I'm talking about people who are listening for mistakes, hoping you slip up, so they can use your failings to prove their own superiority.

Take the people who attack others for saying "I feel good" instead of "I feel well." Yes, it's more precise to say "I feel well" than it is to say "I feel good." But does that really mean that "I feel good" is wrong?

Not exactly.

Someone who thinks "I feel good" is universally wrong is likely the victim of some dust-covered relic of an English teacher who hasn't opened a dictionary since they were written with dodo feathers.

The truth is that today some dictionaries include a definition of "good" as "healthy, strong, vigorous" or "free from injury or disease." In other words, "good" can be nearly synonymous with "well."

Of course, dictionaries are designed mainly to tell us how the language is used, not how it should be used. That's how "wrong" words eventually become right and why some people question dictionaries' authority.

So keep that in mind while weighing whether it's worth getting in a fight over "I feel good." Your time might be better spent telling AOL or Fox News the opinions they so desperately want to hear.

3

I feel <u>well</u>.

This usage is: **Also correct.**

I know. I know. How cruel can the language be? Fresh from hearing that "I feel good" and "I feel bad" are both acceptable, now you're hearing that "I feel well" is fine, too.

So we'll blow through this one quickly and I swear I'll never bring up constructions with "I feel" again (until, of course, we get to the cluster of twenty-eight chapters about my cats, for whom I feel so very, very much).

Here's the thing you need to remember about "well": It's an adverb, most commonly described as an adverbial form of "good"—"I am good at math, so in math I do well." But it's also an adjective, a completely distinct word meaning "in good health." (It's some other stuff, too, including a noun meaning a deep pit from which to fetch stinky water, but here we'll set all other such meanings aside.)

So yes, as we saw, the copular "feel" takes an adjective—"bad"—as its complement: "I feel bad." But when talking about your health by saying "I feel well," the word "well" *is* an adjective.

That's why "I feel well" is fine. And that's all I have to say about that.

4

This is between you and I.

This usage is: Wrong.

Good news. Wonderful things are about to happen to me. I know this because a friend just forwarded me an e-mail saying that if I forward it to others, I can expect "a very pleasant surprise."

In fact, the e-mail includes an impressive, elaborate chart estimating the returns I can expect on my e-mail–forwarding investment: Send to zero to four people, this document tells me, and "your life will improve slightly." Send to five to nine people and "your life will improve to your liking." This goes on all the way up to fifteen, at which point "your life will improve drastically and everything you ever dreamed of will begin to take shape."

I considered cashing in my zero-recipient option, sending to no one and just keeping the "your life will improve slightly" benefit as my free gift. But the "everything you ever dreamed of" stuff is too tempting. I mean, how can I pass up a chance to see Pat Buchanan in a French maid costume wrestling Ricky Martin in a tub of expired yogurt and tequila worms?

The content of the message, by the way, is a list of pithy little life tips like "Open your arms to change. But don't let go of your values." They're credited to the Dalai Lama, though methinks me smells the guiding hand of Dr. Phil.

So I'm sending this e-mail, titled "Good Karma," to the first fifteen e-mail addresses on the "contact our staff" list at the Christian Coalition website.

Now we play the waiting game.

Day one: Nothin'.

Day two: Nothin'.

Day three: No Pat. No Ricky. Just a frightened-sounding e-mail from Ralph Reed wondering if karma could be for real.

Day four: I give up.

Too bad, because not only would the "everything you've ever dreamed of" promise have quenched my thirst for homoerotic Buchanan-based entertainment, but it also would have put an end, once and for all, to people's use of "between you and I."

People who say "between you and I" are still stuck in a time when their mothers scolded them for saying, "Bobby and me are going to the movies." But just because Mom was right that time doesn't mean that every "Bobby and" must be followed by an "I." Ditto for constructions with "you and."

The easy way to always get this right is to just plug in another pronoun in its subject and object forms. Remember that "I" is a subject, "me" an object. "He/she" are subjects, "him/her" are objects. "We" is to "us" as "they" is to "them." And "you" is the oddball, identical as both subject and object—so don't use that one.

So, plugging in "we" and "us," ask yourself which sounds better: "between we" or "between us"? No-brainer, right? It's the object "us." That's why "between you and me" is correct and "between you and I" is incorrect.

It also helps to note that "between" is a preposition and prepositions take objects. Thus, the pronoun that follows should be in the form of an object, "me," and not a subject, "I."

It's not so cut-and-dried with the "Bobby and me" and "Bobby and I" choices because you don't always have a preposition hanging around to tip you off. In these cases, you have to determine whether you need a subject or an object. To be sure, just drop the "Bobby and" to see whether "I" or "me" works best in the sentence: "Bobby and I go to the movies" because it's "I go to the movies," not "Me go to the movies," and it's "You can come with Bobby and me" because it's "You can come with me" and not "You can come with I."

Now go forth and forward this wisdom to at least fifteen others, telling them to do the same. It won't make all your dreams come true, but it'll sure help with one of mine.

5

I <u>could care</u> less.

This usage is: An error, but less so every day.

I could care less about this usage.

I mean that.

If I cared about this expression as much as I care about, say, football or TomKat or songs about "lovely lady lumps," that would definitely be less. A lot less. That's because I could *not* care less about football or celebrity pairings or songs about rear ends I myself can never hope to sport.

But when it comes to this expression, I care a little. Not as much as the scary snobs who pounce on this mistake like a lioness on a gazelle, but a little. Here's their bloodthirsty beef, which is probably apparent already:

"I could not care less" means you care so little that it's inconceivable that you could give less of a hoot. But for some reason there's an increasing tendency among speakers, writers, and a certain princess-like columnist who shall here remain unnamed to slip up and leave out the "not" or the "n't" part of the contraction. The result, of course, is that we—I mean they—end up saying the exact opposite of what they mean.

"I could care less" means you care some. This is the attitude you should take about this expression showing up in your own speech and writing. "I couldn't care less" means you give nary a fig. This is the attitude you should take when some other poor, innocent, lovely, momentarily weak person flubs this expression.

Of course, the "I could care less" version has become so widely used that some linguists now say it's a full-fledged idiom—an accepted common expression. But use it and some will call you a full-fledged idiot.

6

I could **of** turned out worse.

This usage is: Wrong.

$\mathcal{B}$ack before I knew anything about the hazards of grammar snobbery, before I'd learned to resist the gleeful rush that comes with spotting someone else's language ignorance, I noticed someone close to me making this mistake.

It was typed, of course. Not spoken. When spoken aloud, the incorrect "could of" sounds exactly like the correct "could've." That's why people make the error in the first place. "Could have," "should have," and "would have" all pose the same danger—a chance for your ear to lead you astray.

Anyway, I regret to admit that my acquaintance's error lingered in my memory as evidence of this person's . . . um . . . less-than-brilliance. To this day, this mistake still rouses a beast within me. Luckily, I've since learned that I'm not the only person who has reacted this way. Indeed, this is one usage that the grammar cops love to clobber.

"I hate hate hate it when people say somebody 'could of' done something or 'would of' said something," writes a user named Deb on a message board at the Sleeping Baby Productions website. "I could HAVE chewed nails every time I read that, and I would HAVE said something about it were I not convinced doing so would start a flame war."

Obviously, my advice is to avoid such wrath by making sure you know your stuff. Luckily, on some level, you already do.

For example, you might say, "I have seen the light," or even, "I've seen the light." But you wouldn't say, "I *of* seen the light."

That's because you already know quite a bit about auxiliary verbs—whether you know you know it or not. Auxiliaries are often called helping verbs because that's what they do. In "I have danced the tango many times," the word "have" is acting as an auxiliary—allowing us to conjugate "dance" in a way that indicates time and duration.

There are two basic kinds of auxiliaries: primary and modal. Primary auxiliaries are a small group. *The Oxford English Grammar* lists only three: "be," "have," and "do":

> "I am going" uses a conjugated form of "be."
> "George hasn't arrived" uses a conjugated and negative form of "have."
> "Sarah didn't RSVP" uses a conjugated and negative form of "do" as something called an "operator."

Basically, this is all simple stuff you get right every day without opening a single grammar book.

But "modal auxiliaries" are a little trickier. They include: "can," "could," "may," "might," "shall," "should," "will," "would," "must," and some others.

Notice that "could," "should," and "would" all show up on this list. These modal auxiliaries have a special job above and beyond that of the primary auxiliaries. They tell you something about either the *factuality* of what's being said or *human control* over it.

In "I could eat this whole cake," the modal "could" makes reference to my incredible cake-eating ability (human control). In

"Joe may be at the party," the modal "may" tells us that it's not certain that Joe will be there (factuality).

In more complex conjugations, modals team up with the primary auxiliary "have" to shed more light on the "when." "I could dance all night" tells you that you're in for an exhausting evening. "I *could have danced* all night" makes it clear I'm talking about something in the past.

Auxiliaries are just the tools that we use automatically in these situations—these conjugations that necessarily take a form of "have." And that's why "could of," "should of," and "would of" just don't cut it.

Merriam-Webster Online, the only source I know that even mentions the possibility of using "of" in this way, makes its feelings quite clear: "*Of*: nonstandard [for] *have*—used in place of the contraction *'ve* often in representations of uneducated speech."

And that's why I should *have* been a little more understanding.

7

*I*t's so fun to say "so fun" in front of people who are too darn sure it should be "so much fun" (that is, people who are no fun). And trust me, there are a lot of them out there.

"My pet peeve [is] 'It was so fun,'" wrote a user at the Scrapjazz website. "It just doesn't make sense in a grammatical sense."

Well, that depends on which authority you listen to.

According to traditional, tried-and-true usage, most authorities agree that "so much fun" is definitely better. But that doesn't mean you can't get away with "so fun."

This all has to do with the fact that, traditionally, "fun" is a noun.

Think of another noun—say, "milk"—and it's clear why you can have "so much milk" but you can't say something is "so milk."

There's only one problem: Dictionaries, linguists, and usage guides all allow some elbow room on using "fun" as an adjective. The reason: Unlike "mirth," "glee," "joy," and many other nouns of emotion, "fun" doesn't have a corresponding adjective. You can have a mirthful personality, a gleeful attitude, or a joyous day, but you can't have a funful personality or funnous day. That's why some grudgingly allow "It was a fun day" as well as "This day was so fun."

And that's why *Garner's Modern American Usage* allows it as a "casualism." *Fowler's Modern English Usage* doesn't like it, but acknowledges that it's gaining some respectability. And *Webster's New World College Dictionary* and *The American Heritage Dictionary* both include "fun" as an adjective with the caveat that it's "informal."

So is it really so horrible that slackers abusing the language have misused "fun" as an adjective for so long that it's now accepted as an informal usage? Or is this just a case of logic and practicality trumping an unnecessary restriction? I don't know. But it's a fun question.

But learning this is even <u>funner</u>.

This usage is: Very unwise.

*F*unner has no friends. Unlike its pretty, popular sibling "fun," which gets invited to all the noun parties and even gets to join in the adjective games, funner is doomed to a life of sitting home on Saturday nights, hoping against hope to someday get the call from Webster, Garner, or Fowler that will signal its long-awaited admission to the "in crowd." (Not likely, considering that James Kilpatrick says of "funner" and "funnest": "Strangle them.")

You may be tempted to take pity on poor funner. After all, so many other adjectives have what are called "comparative" and "superlative" forms. Its close cousin "funny," for example, boasts "funnier" and "funniest." So you might find yourself wanting to invite funner into an occasional memo or e-mail. But this wouldn't be doing funner or yourself any favors. Funner must learn to accept reality: No dictionary, no usage guide, no half-baked small-town-newspaper style book is on its side.

But don't feel too bad. Funner isn't exactly noble in defeat. It spends those lonely Saturday nights picking on the only member of the family even less likely to ever be accepted as a word: the superlative "funnest."

9

Will everyone who's annoyed by this sentence please raise <u>their</u> hand?

This usage is: Risky.

Will everyone who's annoyed by this sentence please raise their hand? Now, will everyone who prefers *this* sentence please raise his or her hand? Will everyone who prefers *this* sentence, the status quo, and monster truck rallies please raise his hand? And will everyone who prefers *this* sentence, the paintings of Georgia O'Keeffe, and shoe fashions by Birkenstock now raise her hand?

Good. Now that your hands are in the air you'll find it harder to operate a machine gun, a hand grenade, or—the most dangerous weapon of all—your computer keyboard. And no doubt all of you who cared enough to raise a hand will now want to reach for at least one of those as I deliver the horrible news about pronoun agreement.

The biggest misperception about grammar is that it's a system of clear rules—right and wrong. Most people like to believe that grammar is cut-and-dried and rigid enough to offer unimpeachable rulings on the correctness of any given sentence. And that just ain't so.

Grammar keeps changing. "Right" and "wrong" keep changing, and some of the most esteemed grammar books, such as *The Oxford English Grammar* and *The Cambridge Grammar of the English Language*, are written by adherents to the "descriptivist" perspective that usage—even misusage—determines correctness.

Take, for example, the use of "their" to refer back to "everyone." A lot of people, some quite cranky, are inclined to believe that grammar rules render this usage wrong. "Their" and "they" refer to plural subjects. John and Jessie sold *their* house. *They* wanted to move to the beach. "Everyone," on the other hand, is usually singular. (If you're not so sure about that, ask yourself if you prefer "Everyone *is* going to the beach" or "Everyone *are* going to the beach.") Ditto for "everybody," "anyone," "anybody," and "somebody."

So, from this perspective, a sentence such as "Everyone raise their hand" is a case of mortal syntax because the plural "their" has the singular antecedent "everyone."

A piece written for the Cox News Service is a good example of the ire this usage raises: "'Each boy brought their book to class' is NOT right," Elizabeth Schuett wrote for the news service. "Aaagh! Just writing the words gives my clenched jaw a charley horse."

Unfortunately for Schuett, these usages are on the rise—big time. As a result, "right" and "wrong" on this issue aren't as simple as they used to be.

"Why is this usage becoming so common?" asks Bryan Garner in *Garner's Modern American Usage.* "It is the most convenient solution to the single biggest problem in sexist language—the generic masculine pronoun."

Sure, you could use "his or her" instead. You could also recast the sentence. But sometimes those options are pretty unattractive, especially when a snappy little "their" will get the job done so neatly.

Garner calls this use of "their" sloppy and a bad idea, but not even he is willing write it off as a universal no-no.

"Where noun-pronoun disagreement can be avoided, avoid it," Garner writes. "Where it can't be avoided, resort to it cautiously because some people may doubt your literacy."

That's a middle-of-the-road position. Far to the one end of the spectrum, *New York Times* style flat-out forbids "their" to refer to everyone, anyone, etc. Crabby columnist James Kilpatrick agrees, pointing out that he and the *Times* are pretty much the only ones left.

At the other end of the spectrum, linguists like University of California at Santa Cruz professor and author Geoffrey Pullum defend a more liberal interpretation. "Singular 'they' is becoming completely standard, at least among younger Americans, whenever the antecedent is of a sort that could in some contexts refer to either sex."

So in Schuett's example, "their" is indeed a bad choice because it refers to "each boy." Here, a simple "his" will do just fine. If the example were "Each *child* brought their book to class," it would make a lot more sense to ditch "his" for "their." But perhaps the most sensible choice of all is to avoid this situation entirely whenever possible.

10

I <u>have got</u> in trouble over "got."

This usage is: Two different usages, both of which you can get away with but neither of which is advised.

As a resident in good standing of Southern California, I regularly observe Los Angeles County's mandatory weekend evacuation to Las Vegas. Officials keep secret the exact process by which they, on a rotating basis, select evacuees. But it's clearly done through some kind of high-tech surveillance of residents' brain patterns. The minute we get so fed up with traffic and smog that we'd almost consider voting in a local election, officials send a powerful radio-wave impulse into our brains that tells us to sit in our cars for five hours on the road to the land of Coca-Cola museums and Celine Dion concerts. We return home so overstimulated from Canadian circuses and adult-themed tribute acts with names like Danny Glans that we don't have the cognitive function to vote even on *American Idol.*

I love Las Vegas, but in a very conflicted way. I enjoy games like blackjack, but I don't enjoy handing twenty-dollar bills to a woman named Shirley who invests four hundred dollars a month in manicures but whose employer invests zero dollars a month in a dental plan. If I could find fifty-cent-a-hand blackjack in one of the nicer hotels (say, any whose headlining act wasn't a roach circus or a Pia Zadora impersonator), I'd play there. But until the Four Seasons Las Vegas gets smart about how to part me from eight to ten of my hard-earned dollars, I'll continue to spend entire weekends in Sin City without gambling a single penny.

I've found plenty of other ways to entertain myself there. Here's a favorite you can try: Stand in the casino watching some alcoholic Harley-Davidson dealer from Tulsa play hundred-dollar-a-hand blackjack. When, after twenty minutes, he's walking away flat broke, say, "Ha ha! I've got more money than you even though I'm just a lowly Corolla driver."

You'd think this could get dangerous, but in fact it's considerably safer than using the same words in the presence of a grammar snob. You see, "I've got" and "I have got" are fighting words. Here's how they work.

"Have got" is two different things.

It's a past form of "get" (called the present perfect tense for those keeping score at home): "I have got in trouble for using got."

But "have got" is also an informal expression meaning "have." "You've got mail" is identical in meaning to "You have mail."

The first one is tricky because American English prefers "gotten" over "got" as a past participle: "I have gotten into trouble." So when putting "get" in past forms, you'd probably be wise to stick to "gotten." But that doesn't mean "got" is wrong. It's just a little more British, that's all.

The expression "You've got mail," a shortened form of "You have got mail," is a whole different thing. Many say it's both illogical and ungrammatical. If "You have *got* mail" means the exact same thing as "You *have* mail," the "got" adds nothing.

But as I said, "have got" is idiomatic. A figure of speech. And as such, it's defended by a lot of usage experts who point to countless fine writers who have used it. That's true despite the fact that *The Oxford English Dictionary* has called it "colloquial or vulgar."

Columnist and author Barbara Wallraff makes an interesting point about "have got." For a question like "How much money have you got?" you wouldn't save any syllables by ditching "got." You'd have to rework your sentence into something like, "How much money do you have," inserting a little "do" to do got's job.

So, yes, you can get away with saying "I've got into trouble for taunting gamblers" instead of "I've gotten." And you can also get away with saying "I've got to scope out the exits before taunting drunken gamblers" instead of "I have to scope out the exits." But if you've got no stomach for risk, you've got to ask yourself whether it's worth it.

11

I wish I **was** taller.

This usage is: A bad call.

In a classic *Seinfeld* episode, Elaine publishes a cartoon in the *New Yorker*. Though we never see the cartoon, the characters divulge that in it, a pig standing in a complaints line says to a clerk, "I wish I was taller." Hilarity ensues as the rest of the gang wonders why that's supposed to be funny and as Kramer suggests a different complaint for the pig—one not very flattering to the pig's wife.

Not to diminish the sufferings of short swine with promiscuous spouses, I too have a wish I'd like to level at some divine complaint counter in the sky: I wish I could magically help everyone in the world to understand the subjunctive. But, as I've written before, the subjunctive is messy stuff. For one thing, though it's slowly fading from the language, parts of it are still hanging on.

The subjunctive is a "mood" most often used with "statements contrary to fact." And because the things we wish for are things that are not yet fact, "I wish" statements take the subjunctive.

Most of the time, using the subjunctive just means changing "was" to "were." That's because in the past tense, "to be" is the only verb that takes the subjunctive. And because the subjunctive past tense of "to be" is "were," it's as easy as changing "was" to "were": "I *was* taller than Mr. Curlytail," but, "I wish I *were* taller than his wife, as well."

Obviously, "you," "we," and "they" already take "were." So the subjunctive in these cases is identical to nonsubjunctive uses—mainly the "indicative," which is the mood we tend to think of as standard for most speech and writing: "You were there" is indicative; "You wish you were there" is subjunctive. "I was there" is indicative. "I wish I were there" is subjunctive.

Other situations also call for the subjunctive. They are: suppositions, especially ones beginning with "if"; demands and commands; suggestions and proposals; and "statements of necessity."

This rule explains why you use the subjunctive in a supposition such as "If she *were* a better wife, her husband would feel taller." It's the reason that "were" isn't "was."

But as the other situations demonstrate, the subjunctive isn't just about changing "was" to "were." Take a demand such as "I insist that he consult a lawyer." Normally, with "he" you'd use "consults." But because this is a demand, it takes the subjunctive. And unlike the past-tense form of the subjunctive, which applies only to "to be" (i.e., "was" to "were"), the present tense of the subjunctive applies to all verbs—in this case, "consult."

To make a subjunctive for a present-tense verb, just use the "base form" of the verb. Think of the base form as the infinitive (naturally, without a "to"): "He consults" becomes "he consult." "He wears" becomes "he wear" in a suggestion such as "I suggest that he wear platform shoes." "She goes" becomes "she go" in a statement of necessity such as "It's crucial that she go to counseling."

Of course, not many people know all this and even those who do sometimes ignore it. So if you remember just one thing about the subjunctive, it should be that for statements contrary to fact, "was" becomes "were." That's why the pig would have been better off wishing he *were* taller.

12

Resources are spread <u>thinly</u>.

This usage is: Wrong.

 wo grammar snobs and a certain lovely columnist walk into a bar. The first grammar snob says to the bartender, "I'd like a drink served strongly." The second grammar snob says to the bartender, "I would like a beer served frothily." The lovely columnist says to the bartender, "It's okay. I'm driving so these two won't turn up on the side of the road deadly."

I know, I know. It's funny *and* it makes you think.

This brilliant joke was inspired by a real-life National Public Radio reporter whose name I didn't catch. He was interviewing a worker whose job I don't remember about a subject I wasn't quite clear on. (These journalistic skills brought to you courtesy of ten years working in the exciting world of low-paid community news reporting.) Here's the thing I did catch: At one point, the NPR reporter asked the worker whether sometimes resources "get spread more thinly." A few minutes later, the worker mentioned that, yes, resources often "get stretched thin."

This brings us to perhaps the single most important thing to know about grammar: Whenever applying a "rule" that feels awkward and unnatural, it's probably wrong. Listen to your ear and your instincts. That's what our NPR reporter should have done. That's why, by minding his p's and q's too carefully, the reporter flubbed a usage that a man who doesn't work with words got right without even trying.

The principle here is the same as the one we read about in chapter 1. That is, verbs don't always take adverbs. Often, what you want is not a word to describe the action but a word to describe the noun. You want an adjective.

In this example, "thin" is being used not to describe the action of spreading but to describe the state of the subject. You're saying the resources are thin (an adjective), not that the person who spread them out went about doing so in a thin manner (which would require an adverb).

Garner's Modern American Usage puts it better: "'Chop the onions fine' does not describe the manner of chopping but the things chopped." Ditto, Garner notes, for meat sliced "thin" (not "thinly") and "open your mouth wide" (not "widely"). In other words, these situations call for adjectives.

So if you ever find yourself sitting in a bar next to a snob ordering "a drink served strongly" or "a beer served frothily," feel free to beat him senseless. And know that you're not beating him senselessly.

13

I feel sick, so I'm going to <u>lay</u> down.

This usage is: Wrong.

*I*n the past, while writing about the difference between "lie" and "lay," I have found it impossible to restrain my inner Beavis and Butthead. Today, I'm here to demonstrate the newfound maturity and dignity with which I now explain the difference between these two perfectly respectable words.

Lay is a transitive verb, which means it takes an object: "I lay the blanket on the ground."

"Lie" (as in reclining, not as in prevaricating) is an intransitive verb. It's something you do to yourself: "I lie on the ground."

The stinker here is that the past tense of "lie" just happens to be "lay": "Today I lie on the ground. Yesterday I lay on the ground."

Annoying, I know. But this one's worth the effort because it's on so many grammar cops' hit lists. Just memorize these inflections and you'll have no problem:

lie/lay/lain
lay/laid/laid

"Lie" has the past tense "lay" and the past participle "lain." If you're rusty on the terminology, just think of the past participle as the one that goes with "have" in constructions such as "I have lain." The transitive verb "lay" has the past tense "laid" and its past participle is also "laid." (Heh-heh, heh-heh. She said "laid.")

(Yeah, and you know what else? Check out chapter 3. She said "copular feel." Heh-heh.)

(Yeah. That's cool.)

14

The media is biased.

This usage is: Skunky but defensible.

*L*et's say, hypothetically speaking, that you're an extremist ultraconservative Republican just out of journalism school. (I'll pause here to wait for you to stop laughing. Done? Good. Moving on . . .)

You get your first reporting job at a newspaper in San Francisco. Your first day on the job you run out and do a big story on why we should nuke the IRS. Your next day on the job you produce an excellent piece about why not just school prayer but home prayer should be mandatory nationwide. On day three you land exclusive interviews with scholars who can demonstrate that society would be better off if we locked up all single mothers, put their children in factories manufacturing little stickers that say "Made in Taiwan," and renamed America "Ronaldreaganica." On your fourth day, at long last, you receive journalism's highest honor, the "I Enlightened the Ignorant Masses and Showed Them Their Opinions Were All Wrong" Award.

That's one possibility.

Here's another: Maybe you instinctively know that, to keep your job, you have to aim your coverage toward the center—that is, due left. And, despite these efforts, people keep accusing you of media bias, so you skew further and further to the left in hopes of finding that middle ground, perhaps even overcompensating.

You overcompensate so much that you find yourself actually referring to Bill Clinton as "the former president" instead of "Devil on the Blue Dress." And maybe—just maybe—you do so not just to keep your job but because you actually believe in the journalistic principle of fairness.

(Sorry to get so far off topic, but I get a little cranky whenever I see or hear the words "media bias"—even when I'm the one who used them. I've been this way ever since a Newport Beach reader accused me of writing a "socialist diatribe" because he thought one of my articles was too sympathetic toward a yacht club. That's right, a yacht club. When I wrote him back to say that was ridiculous, he conceded that the s-word didn't apply. Then we were finally able to open a dialogue on what we agreed was the real culprit: crappy reporting.)

Anyhoo, now we can move on and get to the important question at hand, which is: Is it okay to use the singular verb ("The media is biased") instead of the plural verb ("The media are biased")?

Most of us know that "media" is the plural of "medium," just as "data" is the plural of "datum," and "bacteria" is the plural of "bacterium." So all these plurals need plural verbs, right? Right?

Well, not necessarily.

"When a word undergoes a marked change from one use to another," Bryan Garner writes, "it's likely to be the subject of dispute."

These "skunked terms," as they're called, tend to divide people into two camps: those who think you're prissy if you stick to the old usage and those who think you're dumb if you opt for the new one. In other words, skunked terms are a lot like media bias: If you look hard enough, you'll find something that stinks—whether it exists or not.

But a little-known fact is that there is a third contingent—a group I like to call "reasonable people," who have better things to do than nitpick your every word or scour community newspapers for Stalinist pro-yacht-club conspiracies.

"Media—as a shortened form of communications media—is increasingly used as a mass noun: 'The media was overreacting,'" Garner writes. "While that usage still makes some squeamish, it must be accepted as standard."

But Eric Partridge's 1942 *Usage and Abusage* and Theodore Bernstein's 1965 *The Careful Writer* disagree, saying "media" is always plural. The more recent *Chicago Manual of Style* also supports this rule.

Bill Walsh, *Washington Post* copy desk dude and author of *The Elephants of Style* and *Lapsing into a Comma*, agrees with Garner.

Fowler's allows you to treat "media" as either a plural or a singular, but adds: "When in doubt, use the plural."

And that's why these terms are so skunky.

Note that most agree that, when you're talking about clairvoyants, the plural is "mediums," but that no such exemptions apply in artspeak: An artist works in various "media"—not "mediums."

One more thing. "Skunked terms" aren't limited to agreement issues but also include definitions in flux, such as "effete," "decimate," and "enormity." For all these words, all you can do is pick your polecat.

15

It's <u>an</u> historic moment.

This usage is: The completely defensible choice of obnoxious poseurs everywhere.

*A*s I mentioned in the Introduction, this book is not about my personal opinions on usage. I don't make rules. The language has too many self-appointed dictators already. My job is just to help you navigate the "rules" already out there.

That's why I consider it my duty to set aside my personal feelings and give you a fair and balanced reporting on the choice between "a historic" and "an historic."

"A historic" is the choice of many smart, cool, unpretentious people because "a," we all know, goes before a consonant sound. "An historic" is the choice of many stuffy, uptight poseur types who fall back on one of two arguments to defend their positions. Some of these ridiculously haughty types prefer "an" because, they say, the "h" in historic isn't pronounced at all. Slightly less absurd members of this grandiose camp say that it's not about consonant sounds but about the stress on the syllables. Because the first syllable of "historic" is not stressed, they say that the "h" sound, while there, sort of gets buried.

So, who's right—the reasonable people or the pseudoliterary goofballs trying their darndest to sound like they just stepped out of a Jane Austen novel?

Why, both choices are right. The good one and the terrible one.

All-around cool guy Mark Twain said of "humble," "heroic," and "historical": "Correct writers of the American language do not put 'an' before these words."

Some linguist named Dwight Bolinger—who I'd never heard of but who sounds cool enough to me—called people who use "an" before "historical" guilty of: "Cockneyed, cockeyed, and half-cocked ignorance and self-importance."

The Associated Press Stylebook seems to prefer "a" before "historic." *The Chicago Manual of Style* also says that's the way to go. Authorities like Eric Partridge, Bryan Garner, *Fowler's* third edition author R. W. Burchfield, Bill Walsh, and Theodore Bernstein all either prefer or openly advocate "a."

But all this overwhelming evidence as to why "a" is better doesn't mean that "an" is wrong.

Feel free to use the ridiculous, goofy, uptight "an historic" anytime you want to sound like an insufferable blowhard. Your choice is every bit as defensible as, say, Bo Diddley or George Thorogood belting out for an audience of cheering fans, "Whom do you love?"

And there you have it: an unbiased grammatical assessment fair and balanced enough for Bill O'Reilly himself.

16

I get paid <u>biweekly</u>, so
I get two paychecks a week.

This usage is: Best avoided.

Warning: This chapter is not recommended for everyone. Certain people, including those with heart conditions, anger-management issues, or poor bladder control should consult a doctor before reading. Those whose interest in learning better English only slightly outweighs their interest in *Gilligan's Island* should avoid this chapter altogether, lest they become disgusted and never venture to learn another thing about usage ever again that doesn't end with the words "Little Buddy." If, while reading this chapter, you experience dry mouth, increased blood pressure, or the need to punch a reference librarian, discontinue use immediately and consult your bartender.

Here's the deal: A lot of us believe that "bi" should mean "every two" and not "twice per" (insert your own Anne Heche joke here). We have a perfectly good prefix for "twice per": "semi." Therefore, logic and usage suggest, your "biweekly" paycheck comes "semimonthly" (approximately). And that should be the end of the discussion, right?

Perhaps, in a perfect world where "flammable" and "inflammable" weren't synonyms, this would be true. Unfortunately, this just isn't the world we live in. (Final warning to all those now clutching their hearts and yelling, Fred Sanford–style, to deceased relatives: Stop reading now.)

There's some dispute on this issue, but according to some very respected authorities, "biweekly" means not only once every two weeks, but also twice a week. "Bimonthly" means once every two months, but at least as often it's used to mean twice a month. "Semi-annual" means twice a year, but so sometimes does "biannual."

In other words, time periods modified with "bi" and "semi" are a great big huge mess.

Fowler's Modern English Usage tells us, "'bi-'. This prefix, which was first used in contexts of time ('biweekly,' 'bimonthly,' 'biyearly,' etc.) in the 19th century, is a cause of endless confusion. Each compound can mean 'occurring or continuing for two __,' 'appearing every two __,' or 'occurring twice a __.'"

The Careful Writer, Usage and Abusage, Webster's New World College Dictionary, and *The Chicago Manual of Style* offer equally distressing assessments on the ambiguity of "bi." Others try to push logic as fact. For example, *AP* and *Garner's* both say that "biweekly" is every two weeks and "semiweekly" is twice a week. But until the experts and the masses concur, the rest of us should heed the words of Wallraff: "*Bi-* is useless for making clear a rate of recurrence."

Consider using clearer terms like "twice a week" or "every two weeks" instead.

17

I did it <u>on accident</u>.

This usage is: Not recommended.

*C*hildhood, we all know, is rife with accidents. There was the time when I was four years old and I "handed" my sister a pair of scissors from my perch on the top bunk. There was the time I conducted a scientific experiment to determine the contents of her clown punching bag using only my keen observational abilities and a long needle. (Hypothesis: It's full of candy. Findings: Hypothesis disproved.) There was the time when I couldn't hold out long enough to make it to the potty after first-period calculus.

While adulthood isn't immune from accidents (I'm looking at you, Mel Gibson), childhood is the time when we learn the rules and boundaries of the world around us and the limits of our parents' energy to stop us from playing in traffic.

No doubt, this is why kids have so many opportunities to talk about accidents and therefore why they're so prone to driving grown-ups nuts by saying "on accident" instead of "by accident." And certain grown-ups don't like this, not one little bit: "I hate when people say they did something 'on accident,'" a user wrote at the Real Police Forum website. "The correct usage is 'by accident.'"

Unfortunately for the rest of us grown-ups, the authors of language books either aren't as accident-prone or aren't as likely to have kids (which, now that I think about it, is probably a result of not being accident-prone). Either way, they're alarmingly oblivious to the issue.

None of the usage books in my arsenal offers a shred of guidance. *Garner's Modern American Usage, Fowler's Modern English Usage, Lapsing into a Comma, The Complete Idiot's Guide to Grammar and Style, The Chicago Manual of Style, The Associated Press Stylebook*, Strunk and White's *The Elements of Style*, and *The Dictionary of Disagreeable English* are all mum on the subject.

So all we can do is open a dictionary.

In its definition of "accident," *Webster's* gives the example "by accident" but not "on accident."

But when I look up the word "on," I see a few definitions that might be used to construct a case (however flimsy) for "on accident." These definitions of "on" include, "having a basis of or having its ground in (something specified) [based on her diary; on purpose]" and "connected with as a part or member [on the faculty]" and "in the state or condition of [on parole, on fire]."

See them? There are a number of ways for a defender of "on accident" to make his case. Especially because "on purpose" is an example used in the dictionary.

Of course, most eight-year-olds who say "on accident" aren't researching the semantics in order to construct a logical defense of this choice. So you're free to tell them, "It's not 'on accident.' It's 'by accident.'" But your time might be better spent finding a good hiding place for the scissors.

PART II

Adverb Adversity

18

That horse runs <u>real slow</u>.

This usage is: Not pretty, but not ungrammatical either, some say.

*F*or me, there are two standards for good grammar: the grammar I expect from myself (flawless except for all the flaws) and the grammar I expect from everybody else (Excuse me, waitress. I couldn't help but notice that you said, "I ain't got no fives so I's gots to make your change outta all ones." Well, I'm a grammar book author, so I hope you don't mind me telling you that you should change "ones" to "twenties.").

And nothing illustrates my grammatical double standard better than adverb issues like, "That horse runs real slow."

I, for one, am not going to say that something runs "real slow"—not a car, not a horse, not the brain of Paris Hilton. (She could be faking, you know. We'll find out when she gets back here with my change.) I'm going to say they run really slowly.

That's because, as we all know, adverbs modify verbs like "run" as well as adjectives and other adverbs. So the "ly" adverbial forms certainly sound better: The horse runs really slowly.

But does that mean I can criticize others for saying that something runs "real slow" or that a plane "flies direct" or that a fitness nut likes to "eat healthy" or that a professional writer must "live cheap"?

Nope.

The experts all permit at least some adverbs stripped of their "ly," though these experts run the gamut from grudgingly accepting to wildly permissive.

On one end of the spectrum, you have *The Oxford English Grammar* noting that "In informal American English, 'real' and 'sure' are commonly used as intensifiers." For other tail-less adverbs, *Oxford* adds a little less warmly that uses like "They sing terrible" and "You don't talk proper" are "nonstandard forms."

On the other end of the spectrum, you have experts like columnist Jan Freeman arguing, "'Eat healthy' isn't missing an adverb; it just happens to have borrowed 'healthy,' the adjective form, to serve in place of 'healthily' or 'healthfully.' That doesn't make 'healthy' an adjective though; it's the job, not the uniform."

In between, all the experts allow "ly"-less forms to varying degrees: Partridge says that "slow," "quick," and "cheap" can all be used as adverbs; Bernstein adds "bright," "loud," "tight," and others to the list; Garner says that "real" is an acceptable adverb to stand in for "very." Fowler and Burchfield agree.

The big difference between them is the amount of caution these experts recommend. In formal writing, you may want to play it safe, sticking to the "ly" forms whenever they don't sound too forced. (For example, even in the most formal circumstances, a professional writer will probably opt for "sitting pretty" over "sitting prettily.")

It's important to note that not all "manner adverbs," that is, adverbs that describe action, end in "ly." "Fast," "right," "wrong," and many other ly-less words are fully sanctioned adverbs.

When in doubt, it can't hurt to check the dictionary, where you'll see that *Webster's* permits "quick" as an adverb, just like "quickly." And "slow" and "real" are fine as adverbs, too, *Webster's* says.

Me, I'll keep using "quickly," "slowly," and "really." But to criticize others for not doing so? Well, that wouldn't be real smart of me.

19

Therefore, those Lolly's people are going to pay.

This usage is: Correct.

*N*ot long ago, I got the following e-mail from a reader named Bill:

> I'll ask your permission to be critical of one or two (perhaps) minor errors in your column of December 27. . . . I was taught, "Never begin a sentence with the word, 'Therefore.'" (Your second paragraph.) My own writing of this sentence would begin "I vow, therefore, as of . . ."

In response, I have procured the following official court document—a little-known lawsuit filed by some disgruntled words against a once-powerful force in the grammar world:

> In the matter of the class action filed by the word "Therefore" and other adverbs ("the Plaintiffs") against Lolly's Inc. (the "Defendant"):

> On May 9, 2007, the Plaintiffs filed with this Court a petition against Lolly's Inc. seeking damages under U.S.G. Civil Code #123SCHLHSRCK alleging defamation. Specifically, the Plaintiffs claimed damages

on two grounds: (1) That, through negligence or malice aforethought, the Defendant led mass numbers of Generation X viewers to a position discriminatory in favor of "ly" adverbs, effectively leading the public to believe that "therefore," "here," "however," "now," "nevertheless," and others members of the class are not adverbs; and (2) That gross omissions in its "Lolly, Lolly, Lolly, Get Your Adverbs Here" theme (created in cooperation with the organization known as Schoolhouse Rock) directly misled viewers into believing that adverbs modify only verbs, adjectives, and adverbs, but never apply to whole sentences.

In the first matter, Counsel for the Defense cited the following lyrics from the Lolly's theme:

How, where, or when,
Condition or reason,
These questions are answered
When you use an adverb.

Counsel for the Defense argued that such lyrics are inclusive of and not discriminatory to numerous adverbs such as "today," "now," "there," and "soon." Counsel cited an example, "I'll see you tomorrow," noting that Lolly's lyrics make clear that "tomorrow" is an adverb because it answers the question "When?"

Expert testimony, however, demonstrated that this portion of the song either never aired or was pre-

cisely timed so as to coincide with cessations in
television viewing that expert witnesses termed "Fran-
kenberry breaks." Thus, the Court rules in favor of
the Plaintiffs.

On the second charge (i.e., that Lolly's failed to make
clear that adverbs can offer commentary on whole
sentences and do not just modify verbs, adjectives, or
other adverbs), the Court also finds for the Plaintiffs,
noting that Lolly's theme song lyrics exclude substan-
tive mention of this fact.

As such, the Court orders Lolly's Inc. to produce and
air, at its own expense, the following theme song
drafted by a court-appointed lyricist.

Therefore, Therefore, Therefore. Get your adverbs here.
Therefore, Thus, However. They're all adverbs here.
They apply to whole sentences, so one thing's clear:
You can start a sentence with almost any word you wish.
Frankly, Hopefully, Truly, Especially—they all work,
But if you think you need "L-Y" then you're a jerk.
Lots of words are adverbs so open your mind.
Otherwise you won't know why you're so "behind."

The production and broadcasting of said theme
shall be considered restitution for Plaintiffs' dimin-
ished earning capacity as well as for damages of
mental suffering. But it shall not necessarily be
considered compensation for a separate suit, filed
by Therefore's spouse, Hereby, alleging loss of
consortium.

The Defendant has filed an appeal based on pending legislation that would allow litigants in such cases to hire private lyricists and to thus replace lyrics Defendant has argued "would gag a goat." But as of the date of this ruling, said legislation is still just a bill.

20

<u>Hopefully</u>, this guy will get a life.

This usage is: Fine in this here 21st century.

*I*n the days when men wore tights and saucy wenches roamed the land, one might have had just cause to chide others for using "hopefully" to mean "I hope." But even then, the only reason one would do so is out of bitterness from a lifetime of not being invited to make merry in yonder glade.

There are a lot of people in the world who love to pounce on this use of "hopefully." Hopefully, this will put an end to it.

For some of them, the problem is they just don't understand adverbs.

"My most hated grammatical error is the overuse of the word 'hopefully,'" Janey, a user posting at a vegan website, wrote. "It's an adverb! For Christ's sake! Quit putting it at the beginning of every sentence!!!"

Obviously, there's nothing wrong with starting a sentence with an adverb. Conveniently, these are called "sentence adverbs" and they're discussed in the next chapter.

Others, like the following man who wrote to me about one of my columns, actually do understand adverbs. They just don't understand why it's a good idea to open a dictionary from time to time:

"June. I noticed that you ended the column by using the adverb 'hopefully' as a substitute for 'I hope that . . .' or 'It is hoped that. . . .' I know you know better than to use substandard English. —Steve"

Once upon a time, "hopefully" meant only "in a hopeful manner," but not "I hope" or "it is hoped." But by the same token, "thou" used to mean "you," and "sun" used to mean "a big thing that revolves around the earth and will someday inflict its wrath upon us" (just as we moderns would define a Fox News satellite).

We can resolve this "hopefully" business once and for all by just opening a few books, starting with the dictionary:

> hopefully. *adv.* 2. it is to be hoped (that). (*Webster's New World College Dictionary*)

Most other authorities will tell you that this "hopefully" is widely used and widely accepted. Those who don't, most notably *Elements of Style* authors Strunk and White and *The Careful Writer* author Theodore Bernstein, are long gone. Hopefully, neither they nor their cause will rise again.

21

<u>More importantly</u>, never work in a place called Melons.

This usage is: 100 percent kosher, as is "more important."

$\mathcal{B}$y the time I was thirty years old, I could count fifty jobs I'd had—more than half of which I'd been fired from. Highlights include a stint as a hospital "reprocessing technician" (a job that consisted exclusively of collecting dirty linens and dishes), a sales "career" involving walking cold into strange offices to try to convince companies to switch long-distance carriers, and two waitressing stints at a Hooters wannabe known as Melons. (Fired twice. Don't ask. Involves booze.)

What does this have to do with you? Well, besides offering hope and inspiration to your pathologically unemployable brother who goes by the nickname "Chronic" ("See, dude, I can like, turn it around anytime I want and do something totally whack like write grammar books"), it also taps into my vast experience crafting complex rational explanations for work-related mishaps: "You see, Mr. Melons Manager, the grabby gentleman with the 'Mustache Rides' T-shirt was too buzzed to be certain I was the one who dumped that plate of hot wings in his lap. More importantly, he was a lousy tipper."

Chances are you're thinking one of two things: (1) What were you doing working in a place like that? or (2) Where is this Melons place and when is happy hour? But there are people in the world who would seize on a third issue: the use of "more importantly" to begin a sentence. Some people really hate that, just as they probably hate "more important," "most important," and "most importantly."

"Nothing good can be said of *more importantly*," writes columnist James Kilpatrick. "The phrase is pompous, stuck-up, swell-headed. It smacks of watch chains and gray spats. It drips with bombast. It oozes with pretension. 'Oh, how importantly am I!'"

Here's another highly opinionated yet misled commentator: "*Most importantly*. Like fingernails on a chalkboard," writes a user at the SEO Black Hat Forum. "It's *most important*, people!"

Don't listen to them. "More importantly" and "more important" are perfectly grammatical ways to begin a sentence, as are "most important" and "most importantly."

Fowler's and *Garner's* say these uses are fine. Barbara Wallraff doesn't think too highly of "most importantly," but she doesn't say it's wrong, either. *The Elements of Style* takes the boldest stance, saying you should avoid "more importantly," though the authors make clear that this is their personal preference and not a rule.

The bottom line is that "more importantly" and "more important" are both perfectly grammatical. That's in part because, as we saw in previous chapters, adverbs' powers go far beyond just modifying verbs. Often, their job is to "express a comment by the speaker or writer," as *The Oxford English Grammar* puts it—a comment that applies to the whole sentence or that applies to and joins two sentences.

> Admittedly, I wasn't the greatest employee.
> Frankly, I had a bad attitude.
> Additionally, that place smelled like oysters.

These are often called sentence adverbs.

In fact, whole phrases can function this way. "First of all," "for example," "in comparison," "after all," "on the contrary," "in addition"—these phrases are all cited by *Oxford* as adverbials that modify whole sentences.

More importantly, this demonstrates that you can use "more important" and "more importantly" anytime you feel like it. And most important, learning this has ensured that I never have to wear pink silk jogging shorts to work ever again (unless I feel like it).

Firstly, they're wrong.

This usage is: Grammatical.

A few points:

Firstly, this is the same basic idea that you saw in the "more importantly" discussion.

Secondly, "firstly" and friends are so widely criticized that I thought they warranted their own chapter.

Thirdly, the choice between "first" and "firstly" is so clearly up to you that *Oxford* writes them as "first(ly)," "second(ly)," "third(ly)," etc., though other style guides disagree. *Fowler's, The Careful Writer,* and *Webster's* all fully support "firstly"; *Chicago, Garner's,* and *Usage and Abusage* all say "first" is better.

Fourthly, it's true that sometimes this "ly" form can sound really bad.

Fifthly, you don't need some grammar snob to tell you that.

Sixth, consistency is important.

7. You didn't need to be told that, either.

<u>However</u>, lies live longer than liars.

This usage is: Correct.

*T*here are people out there who believe that you can't begin a sentence with "however." There are also people out there who believe that pastel stretch pants are a super way to hide mass quantities of cellulite. (Sometimes I miss Pinellas Park, Florida.)

So where do such lies come from? I'm not sure, but I have a theory: They come from liars. And unfortunately, the lies live on long after the liars have been exposed and even after they have repented.

Take William Strunk Jr. According to linguist Arnold Zwicky (if that is his real name), Strunk was spreading this lie (the "however" one, not the stretch pants one) long before he became half of the linguistic crime-fighting duo of Strunk and White.

As Zwicky reported, the then-solo Strunk wrote in the 1918 incarnation of *The Elements of Style*, "*However*. In the meaning *nevertheless*, not to come first in its sentence or clause."

We'll never know where he got this from—whether he was the victim of some earlier liar or he just pulled it straight out of his stretch pants. Either way, by the time E. B. White was sharing Strunk's byline, the original tough talk had been taken down a peg. Strunk's rule suddenly got recast as just an opinion, albeit a pretty self-assured-sounding one: "*However*. The word usually serves better when not in first position."

The idea has to do with the fact that "however" has two basic meanings. The first is roughly equivalent to "nevertheless" or (stretching it a bit) "but." The second is "in whatever manner" or "to whatever degree." Strunk figured that without his divine guidance people would be hopelessly confused by every "however" they encounter.

For example, we might think that a sentence that begins with "However you look at it" might mean "Nevertheless you look at it." And we might think that a sentence like "However, I will consider your suggestion" could mean "In whatever manner I will consider your suggestion."

"However," Strunk figured, was grammatical rocket science, comprehensible only by the sharpest, Strunkiest minds.

But there's one little problem with Strunk's amazing feat of comprehension: He forgot about the comma. You see, in a sentence that uses "however" in the beginning to mean "nevertheless," it's followed by a comma: "However, not all my stretch pants are pastels."

And when it means "in whatever manner" or something similar, it's not followed by a comma: "However you slice it, Strunk's help wasn't helpful."

In my arsenal of experts, almost all agree that there's nothing wrong with starting a sentence with "however." *Fowler's* agrees. Partridge agrees. Walsh agrees. Bernstein agrees. The only one who hesitates on "however" is Garner, who I suspect is suffering from a disorder I hereby dub "Strunkholm syndrome."

Starting a sentence with the "nevertheless" brand of "however," Garner argued, isn't a grammar gaffe. But it is a "stylistic lapse," he says, adding that "but" is "much preferable."

Lovely advice. However, it's just an opinion—an opinion not about grammar or what's proper, just about style.

24

<u>Anyways</u>, I'll see you later.

This usage is: Just don't go there, okay?

I can't tell you that "anyways" is one hundred percent, irrefutably wrong, because the minute I do some linguist with ten times my grammar expertise will say that common usage has rendered it acceptable. But you've got to pick your battles, and I say this one's not worth it.

Using "anyways" can bring you a world of pain from those who are one hundred percent convinced that it is wrong as well as from people who just think it stinks.

"I can't stand when people say 'anyways' instead of 'anyway,'" writes a user named John on a web page titled "The Most Annoying Mistakes in English."

Pros, such as "Grumbling Grammarian" Robert Hartwell Fiske, can be just as unforgiving: "Labeling 'anyways'—like 'anywheres,' 'somewheres,' and 'nowheres'—dialectical, as many dictionaries do, is too kind. Let them label it what it is: uneducated."

Stick with "anyway" and save yourself a lot of trouble.

25

I am <u>continuously</u> watching *Simpsons* reruns.

This usage is: Incorrect unless you suffer from a medical condition known as Simpsonussansinterruptus.

*M*ost people who watch lots of *Simpsons* reruns watch them *continually*. Only someone with a serious, serious problem watches them *continuously*. You're a continuous viewer if you have Homer and Marge blaring from your DVD player 24/7, if you have monitors throughout the house, including in front of the toilet, and if you watch the show even while you're writing a grammar book.

Normal people, however, watch their programs of choice continually. That's because "continuous" means, basically, "uninterrupted." "Continual" means "frequently recurring."

The major style and usage guides all agree on this one: *Chicago*, *AP*, *Garner's*, and *Fowler's*.

Webster's New World College Dictionary emphasizes this distinction while permitting a little overlap. "Continual," *Webster's* says, can be used in place of "continuous" to mean "uninterrupted." But "continuous" can't take "continual's" job of meaning "intermittent."

For my money, *Chicago* puts it best: "What is 'continual' is intermittent or frequently repeated. What is 'continuous' never stops—it remains constant or uninterrupted."

And here's a little bonus you won't find in any of those authoritative books—a mnemonic device to help you remember the difference: "Continuous" has a second "u," which can help you remember a word that also begins with "u": uninterrupted. So, continue-"us" means uninterrupted.

"Continual" ends in "al." So I like to think of an annoying uncle named Al who pops in continually—often showing up at mealtime but graciously leaving just before it's time to do the dishes. Contrast this with the "us" in "continuous" and you'll see that, while we can get away from Al on occasion, there's no getting away from "us."

See? You can watch *The Simpsons* continuously and still retain enough brain function to come up with great stuff like that.

Stay for awhile.

This usage is: Wrong.

Somewhere out there, no doubt, exists some grammarian-quite-contrarian who would argue tooth and nail that it's okay to write "stay for awhile." But he's not in my library. And if he were, I'm quite sure all the other usage books would wait until the lights went out, then beat him until his cover was shredded and his pages were pulp.

Here's the rule on which this beating would be administered:

When following "for," "in," or some other preposition, you want the two-word "a while" ("Stay for a while"). Without that preposition, you need the one-word version: "awhile" ("Stay awhile").

That's because "awhile" is an adverb, but "while," in these constructions, is a noun. If you remember that "for" and "in" are prepositions, and if you remember that prepositions take objects, and if you remember that objects are usually nouns or pronouns, then you see why it makes no sense for this preposition to take an adverb as its object.

You wait "for him." But you can't wait "for happily" or "for soon" or "for therefore."

But if that's too much to remember, just remember that "for," "in," etc., are followed by the two-word "a while." It might help to think of the word "foray." That is, "for" requires a separate "a."

I like Tom Cruise, <u>irregardless</u> of what the critics, the Academy, or the mental health community might say.

This usage is: Icky-poo.

*A*nyone who's reading a language book probably doesn't need to be told about "irregardless," but just in case, here's the deal:

Don't use it. Use "regardless" instead.

If you insist on flouting this advice (say, perhaps in an attempt to drive your English teacher up a wall), then yes, you can take comfort in the fact that "irregardless" does appear in many dictionaries. But rarely does it appear without some judgmental little qualifier like "nonstandard." So it's best just to stick to "regardless."

I'm <u>way</u> too cool to accost a celebrity (unless it's Rob Corddry).

This usage is: Informal but fine.

*A*s I have reported in the past, we Angelenos know our place. The nobodies, which means most of us, must not pester the celebrities. We know that with the privilege of living near fame comes responsibility—like the responsibility to resist the urge to run up to David Carradine at a bar and say, "Let me guess: You're drinking a grasshopper!" Yes, we get to enjoy sights like Fabio driving a Mercedes down Fairfax Avenue as long as we don't pull up next to him and holler, "I can't believe it's not a Beemer!"

Sometimes the celebrities will even put us nobodies to the test. Take Jay Leno. The two—count 'em, two—times I've seen Jay tooling down the 101 Freeway, he was driving an antique car that would turn heads even without a ten-inch chin sticking out the driver's-side window.

So it is with great sadness that I report I'm no longer the picture of a well-behaved LA nobody. My eleven-year streak has ended. Eleven years of things like seeing Dustin Hoffman stand up in a movie theater and managing to choke back the words "Yo, Stretch, down in front"—destroyed. Eleven years of resisting the urge to ask Alice Cooper, "Were you aware that sitting in a restaurant next to your table of boisterous toadies is *my* nightmare?"—down the toilet. Because just a week before writing this, sitting in the very Starbucks where I've managed not to accost Erik Estrada, Joe Rogan, Marcia Cross, Jay Mohr, and the guy who plays Oscar on *The Office*, I pestered a celebrity. Rob Corddry, mere weeks after his farewell segment on Jon Stewart's *The Daily Show*, was just sitting at one of those little wooden tables, acting like a regular person.

I couldn't resist.

"Um, excuse me, Rob?" (That's right, for one unbelievable moment I thought we were on a first-name basis.)

He swung around, only the faintest hint of "Who is this nut?" visible under his otherwise cordial smile.

"Uh, I wrote this book and I'd love to give you a copy," I said, handing him a copy of *Grammar Snobs*.

A gracious thank-you from him. A few mumbled words from me that failed to express just how hard he made me laugh while he was on *The Daily Show*. A failure to realize the absurdity of my autographing a book for him. A very, very quick exit by him. A pang of embarrassment when I realized I'd stolen his pen.

Now I can no longer brag that I'm *way* too cool to accost a celebrity. My only saving grace is knowing that I am way too language-savvy to let a grammar snob tell you how to use "way."

Yes, substituting "way" for "much" or "far" (think of "much too cool" or "far too cool") may sound like slang best left to informal situations. And yes, it may incur the wrath of guys like Fiske: "The widespread (if witless) use of 'way' to mean 'much' or 'far,' 'exceedingly' or 'especially,' reveals how people favor simplicity over precision, easiness over elegance, and popularly over individuality."

But that doesn't mean that "way" is wrong:

> *Webster's:* "*way.* adv. [Informal] away; far; to a consid-
> erable extent or at some distance [way behind]."

So Marge Simpson's observation that "Jim Nabors is way cool" is both grammatically solid and solid evidence that even the best of us can get a little goofy about celebrities.

PART III

Verbal Abuse

29

It is you who <u>is</u> the smart one.

This usage is: Not as good as "It is you who *are* the smart one."

Consider these pairs: "It is I who *am* here" vs. "It is I who *is* here," "It is you who *are* the smart one" vs. "It is you who *is* the smart one," "It is I who *know* the secret" vs. "It is I who *knows* the secret."

Scared because you don't have a clue how to begin to understand which ones are right? Don't be. Everybody's in the same boat. And nobody seems to know whether the verb should agree with the noun or pronoun or whether it should cozy up to "who," which seems to call for a third-person singular verb (i.e., "who is" and "who knows" instead of "who am" and "who know").

But you're about to.

According to Garner, the "who" in these cases necessarily agrees with the noun or pronoun before it. Therefore, in "It was Steve and Sarah who," that "who" is, by default, third-person plural. So because "Steve and Sarah" take "are," the "who" takes "are" as well: "It is Steve and Sarah who *are* ordering the flowers."

But for a single subject, such as "Mike," the "who" takes the same verb form as the subject, Mike: "It is Mike who *is* ordering the flowers."

The issue here, if you want to do further research (bless your heart) is called "relative pronoun–antecedent agreement."

"Who," along with "that" and "which," is part of a group called relative pronouns. The word "antecedent" just means the word or phrase that a pronoun is referring back to. In "Ned went to his church," the possessive pronoun "his" refers to "Ned," therefore, "Ned" is its antecedent. Simple stuff.

But that's just FYI. The important point here is that "who" gets the exact same verb form as whatever it refers to, according to Garner.

So because it's "I *am* here," you would also say, "It is I who *am* here" (not *is*). Because it's "You *are* the smart one," write "It is you who *are* the smart one" (not *is*). One more set: Because it's "I *know* the secret," write "It is I who *know* the secret"; but because it's "He *knows* the secret," write "It is he who *knows* the secret."

Not many experts offer guidance on this matter, so I can't say that this is the consensus. But if you're looking for an answer, you could do worse than to take Garner's word for it.

30

I <u>rifle</u> through my desk.

This usage is: Wrong (and can make you want to reach for a gun).

"*R*ifle" is a word that has always been part of my lexicon. I rifle through my desk. I rifle through my papers. I'll rifle you good if you don't stop dippin' into my moonshine. (Well, that last usage has faded from my speech some since I left the South, along with "pass the grits" and "yee-haw.") So imagine my dismay when, after using "rifle" this way in a column, I got an e-mail from a reader telling me I meant to use "riffle."

So, resisting the urge to rifle that reader but good, I looked it up.

The definitions are hardly cut-and-dried—there's a lot of wiggle room. But the bottom line is that he was right. I should have been using "riffle" all these years.

Webster's New World College Dictionary says "riffle" means, among other things, "to leaf rapidly through (a book, etc.), as by letting the edges or corners of the pages slip lightly across the thumb." And by the way, it rhymes with "sniffle."

For "rifle" we find the definition, "to ransack and rob (a place); pillage; plunder." So it would be quite a stretch to apply this to a book. What's more, this definition of "rifle" says it's only a transitive verb. That means it requires a direct object. So, according to the strictest interpretation, I can rifle my desk, but I can't rifle *through* my desk. I can rifle the neighbor's house, but I can't rifle *through* the neighbor's house. I can get a rifle and hunt down the guy who first pointed this out to me, but that won't change the ugly reality that I've been using "rifle" wrong all these years.

31

Here's how to __gift__ everyone on your list.

This usage is: Defended by dictionaries, despised by usage mavens.

*I*f the world of grammar were a biker bar, using "gift" as a verb would be the equivalent of insulting some big hairy guy's hog.

Uses like "I have a lot of people to gift this year" are considered seriously offensive by certain people—certain scary people. Take Fiske: "Though 'gift' as a verb is an antiquated form, use of it today is nonsense, even offensive."

Conventional wisdom holds that "give" can handle the job all by itself and doesn't need any help from a noun posing as a verb. But if you're the kind of person who would brazenly hit on the old lady of a guy named Eyeball, then perhaps you'd enjoy taking on the bespectacled and pinched-face geeks who perceive the verb "gift" as a thrown-down gauntlet.

Here's what you need to know: Only a handful of the usage guides in my arsenal have entries for "gift." And none of them likes it as a verb. *Fowler's Modern English Usage* says of the verb, "Despite its antiquity (first recorded in the 16 c.) and its frequent use, esp. by Scottish writers, since then, it has fallen out of favour among standard speakers in England, and is best avoided."

Garner's Modern American Usage (emphasis on the word "American") says "gift" as a verb is "much on the rise." But "on the rise" doesn't mean fully sanctioned in Garner's eyes: "English has the uncanny ability," he writes, "to transform nouns into verbs and to revive moribund usages." (For example, checkers's "King me." Or, one that might come in handy at your local biker bar, "Beer me!") Still, Garner warns, "cautious writers may prefer to keep 'gift' as a noun only."

On the other hand, not-so-cautious writers (that is, brazenly confrontational ones) might want to reach for the metaphorical pool cue known as the dictionary and get swinging. *Webster's New World College Dictionary* fully sanctions "gift" as a verb. So does *The American Heritage Dictionary of the English Language,* Fourth Edition, and my dusty old 1955 *Oxford Universal Dictionary.*

Take that, Eyeball.

32

<u>Loan</u> me some money.

This usage is: Opposed by many.

*I*t's nine o'clock in the morning. Maybe eight. I'm in a hotel room in Minneapolis. Or maybe Milwaukee. I'm holding a telephone to my ear, listening to a radio show I'm about to be on. Listeners have language peeves—lots of 'em. And questions, too—tough ones. One is annoyed that people don't know the difference between "loan" and "lend," though she can't really explain the difference herself. "Well, lucky for you," the hosts tell her, "we have a grammar expert on the line."

In the large mirror on the hotel room wall, staring back at me, is our so-called expert—the grammar savior who's about to dazzle and enlighten the entire Midwest metropolis. She has a towel on her head, two different-colored socks on her feet, and a look of terror on her face—due in part to the fact that she doesn't even know what city she's in, much less the difference between "loan" and "lend."

And we're live in three, two, one . . .

Welcome to my *Grammar Snobs Are Great Big Meanies* book tour—a weeks-long whirlwind of taxicabs and terror.

You would think that years' worth of improv classes would have prepared me for these moments. Not so.

It's true that, in improv class, you might find yourself sitting in front of your fellow students, preparing to play an "expert."

When your teacher asks, "Okay, class, what's she an expert in?" and one of them shouts out, "Mad cow disease," humor is sure to unfold precisely because you don't know cud about the topic at hand. When you find yourself asserting emphatically in a French accent that bovine "spongeolololopothy" is a disease that turns human beings into cattle, people laugh precisely because you're shoveling cow pies.

That BS is not going to fly with the inquiring minds of Minneapolis or Milwaukee.

Luckily, I'm not alone in my hotel room. Some real saviors are there with me, in book form, that is. I open *Garner's*.

"Actually, Mr. and Ms. Radio Show Host (I say, or something to that effect), I have an answer to the 'loan'/'lend' question right here. According to *Garner's Modern American Usage* . . ."

The point of this story is that most people who are insecure in their use of the language assume they're supposed to have all the answers in their heads. And I believe that this misperception is one of the biggest hindrances to learning grammar. There's too much to commit to memory. It's too overwhelming, so we give up.

Don't. All you need to know are some fundamentals of grammar—the basics—and where to turn for answers to the specifics.

On the "loan"/"lend" question, many style guides will tell you that "loan" is a noun and "lend" is a verb. When someone lends money, he's making a loan.

Of course, others disagree. Academics, less-rigid style guides like *Garner's*, and the dictionary will tell you that "loan" can be used as a verb, too.

So just be aware that there are two camps. Then, just picture their leaders in their underwear, complete with mismatched socks, shoveling linguistic cow pies.

33

What, exactly, are you <u>inferring</u> about my mother?

This usage is: Wrong, but I say that only because I'm inferring that you mean "implying."

*T*here are a lot of people out there, it seems, who are hopping mad over the rampant confusion about "imply" and "infer." I find this somewhat curious, as I, personally, have never heard anyone confuse these words.

The difference seems pretty straightforward to me. But of course, that may be due to my sitcom-steeped youth in which I heard the punch line "What, exactly, are you implying about my ('mother,' 'manhood,' etc.)?!?" even more often than "What you talkin' 'bout, Willis?" and "Up your nose with a rubber hose."

So for all those sitcom-deprived readers out there, here's the standard explanation, courtesy of a sitcom and paraphrased from fuzzy memory:

> *Homer:* What are you inferring?
> *Lisa:* No, Dad. I imply. You infer.

And for those of you who believe that the advice of TV characters can't measure up to real book smarts: "To 'imply' is to suggest. To 'infer' is to conclude," writes Fiske in *The Dictionary of Disagreeable English*.

Of course, some authorities, most notably *Webster's*, actually allow "infer" to mean "imply." But most won't hear of it:

The writer or speaker "implies" (hints, suggests); the reader or listener "infers" (deduces). Writers and speakers often use "infer" as if it were synonymous with "imply," but careful writers always distinguish between the two.
> —*Chicago* (Well, *careful* writers and sitcom viewers.)

Imply. Infer. Not interchangeable.   —*Strunk and White*

Writers or speakers "imply" in the words they use. A listener or reader "infers" something from the words.
> —*AP Stylebook*

Writers frequently misuse "infer" when "imply" . . . would be the correct word.   —*Garner*

It gives me the willies, personally, when someone uses "infer" to mean "imply"—but as linguists, we have no dog in that fight.   —*Linguist Mark Liberman*

I could go on. But I won't. A *Simpsons* rerun is about to start.

34

The woods were <u>decimated</u> by the fire.

This usage is: In flux.

$\mathcal{T}$here are two reasons to pitch a hissy fit over the evolving meaning of a word. Either you hate to see the word lose its original meaning because it's a useful word with few substitutes, or you just pretend to be offended because that gives you an opportunity to show off your extraordinary genius.

"Literally" is a good example of the former. Slowly, it's gaining credibility as meaning "almost literally" or even "figuratively." And when "literally" means "figuratively," what word will we have to mean "literally"?

"Decimate" is a good example of the latter. Lurking everywhere are people who are really proud that they know the word originates from an ancient practice of killing one in ten soldiers in order to punish the lot.

So whenever they see "decimate" used to mean "devastate," "destroy," "vanquish," "nearly wipe out," or even "wipe out completely," they moan and they whine and they ham it up like a Southern belle having an attack of the vapors.

"The devastation of 'decimate' is my pet peeve," writes a user at TechRepublic.com. "This is an old Latin term that means to kill every tenth person; you could extend it to also kill every tenth animal, but you can not kill a building or a town. . . . The bloody word is 'devastate' or its derivatives. This misuse is so devastating to me, and English teachers everywhere."

Do these people really expect us to believe that we need a word for the deliberate annihilation of one in ten anything? Are they plotting something evil—for example, the systematic destruction of one in ten dictionaries? That's the only thing that would justify their rabid insistence that "decimate" means to kill precisely one in ten and that the word cannot evolve.

But not all objections to "decimate" can be as easily laughed off. There exist two other camps, more reasonable ones, that disagree on how far "decimate" has truly evolved. Some say it can mean any form of destruction, wiping out, or even vanquishing, like "The Panthers decimated the Gazelles in last night's game." But others, and these are the people you should probably listen to, say the best use lies somewhere in between.

"Decimate," they say, can mean "to destroy a large proportion of" but it shouldn't mean "to destroy all of." That's the advice of *Chicago, Fowler's, Garner's,* Partridge, Bernstein, Wallraff, Fiske, and *Webster's New World College Dictionary.* And you can't decimate a consensus like that.

If your nose itches, <u>itch</u> it.

This usage is: Irritating.

*I*f you're the kind of person who finds yourself logging on to the Internet to rant about others' infuriating use of "itch" to mean "scratch," I would like to make a prediction: You will someday buy airport-adjacent real estate, then spend the rest of your life complaining about the noise.

True, there are people in the world who use "itch" to mean "scratch." But let's face it, if you're bothered by them, it means that you're socializing with them—by choice. (And don't give me that "I have no choice: They're my kids!" business. You could have chosen a life of celibacy.)

"Itch" in place of "scratch" is considered "informal" by *Webster's*, is called (get this) "down-market" and "American" by *Fowler's*, and is completely ignored by every other usage expert in my library. In other words, most language-savvy types don't run with these "itch" users and those who do put great effort into distancing themselves from them.

Use this form of "itch" only in one of two situations: (1) You have, on your person, a dictionary that will back you up when someone challenges you (and they will), or (2) Your goal is to be really, really irritating.

I like <u>to mercilessly mock</u> conspiracy theorists.

This usage is: Fine.

Conspiracy theories are bunk. Except when they're true. But even then it's still uncool to admit that you believe them.

Yes, conspiracy theories could explain some otherwise incomprehensible things, like why almost every elected office in the United States is occupied by a member of a bloodline whose males never bald (I'm looking at you, Skull and Bones), or why speculum warmers remain off the medical device market (I'm looking at you, Promise Keepers).

But as a journalist, not to mention someone with a hip image to maintain, I don't believe allegations unless I can back them up with fact (as you'll see in my upcoming documentary, *Who Killed the Electric Ryan Seacrest Doll?*).

That's why I'm here to tell you about so-called "split infinitives" while making clear that there is not—repeat, not—a conspiracy surrounding them. Sure, I could put forth a theory about a cabal of in-the-know educators deliberately trying to make everyone else feel stupid. Sure, I could piece together evidence that the truth about split infinitives is like a holy grail of forbidden knowledge, guarded by a sort of nerdy Knights Templar sporting thick glasses and sensible shoes and who fight to the death to assure that the rest of us continue to believe the hype. But that would be just crazy. Wouldn't it?

Wouldn't it?

There must be some other explanation as to why one of the first things many people learn about grammar is the utterly incorrect "rule" that you can't split an infinitive.

Here's the information most of us have been denied—through no organized conspiracy whatsoever—and which has, purely by coincidence, propelled a select few into elevated positions of knowledge and power.

Basically, there are three schools of thought on splitting infinitives:

> *1.* You can't.
> *2.* You can.
> *3.* You can't—not as in "you may not" but as in "it's impossible because 'to' is not really part of the infinitive in English."

Proponents of option 1 are set apart by one very important trait: Unlike supporters of 2 and 3, these people have probably never read a real grammar book.

An infinitive is the most basic form of a verb—its name. "I danced," "he was dancing," and "they will dance" all use conjugated forms of "to dance," which is the infinitive. When people talk about splitting infinitives, they mean that you can't put anything between the "to" and the other part. And you can shut these people up by opening pretty much any style book available. All the major style guides say in no uncertain terms that you can put anything you like after your "to." Go nuts. "To vigorously shake your pudding." "To happily toss your pasta." "To shamelessly plunder previous chapters for material." Don't give these misinformed anti-split-infinitive pedants another thought.

But even more interesting is a rift between the experts. You see, while many say it's okay to split an infinitive, others say that the "infinitival to" isn't technically part of the infinitive at all.

The base form of a verb—"dance," for example—is the infinitive, they say. "To" is just its helper. So, like all style books, these experts say it's fine to put another word after the "to." They just disagree on whether that constitutes a split.

The Oxford English Grammar agrees that the "to" is not part of a single unit. And no matter how many experts disagree on this point, the important thing is that they all agree it doesn't matter. "Split infinitives" are fine.

So now you can stop worrying about that nonsense and instead turn your attention to more important questions, such as "Why is my presidential ballot stamped with the words 'Property of the Trilateral Commission'?" and most important of all, "Where can I get my electric Ryan Seacrest doll?"

The man <u>spit</u> on the sidewalk.

This usage is: Fine, but so is "spat."

*O*nce upon a time, before I discovered the fine art of doing my homework prior to shooting off my mouth, I used to tell people that they couldn't use "spit" as a past tense.

"It's 'spat,'" I would tell them emphatically.

(In the interest of full disclosure, I should tell you that, in the crowds I ran with, "spit" didn't come up nearly as often as another word that rhymes with it. And I was quite emphatic in my uninformed attempts to enforce usage of "shat.")

Unfortunately for me, I was wrong. Most authorities accept that both "spit" and "spat" are acceptable past tenses for "spit." But they disagree on which is better.

"Avoid 'spit' as the past-tense or past participial form. Despite authoritative support, it sounds dialectical," *Garner's* warns.

Like Garner, *The American Heritage Dictionary* prefers "spat" to "spit" for past tense, but allows both.

The New Fowler's and *Usage and Abusage* remain neutral, saying that both are used in America.

And *Webster's* prefers "spit" to "spat" for the past tense, but allows both.

There aren't as many experts who see the need to weigh in on the rhyming word that contains an "h" in place of the "p." But suffice it to say that it's grammatical in either form in which it might hit the fan.

38

I like to <u>aggravate</u> the easily irritated.

This usage is: Best avoided.

*A*re you tired of having friends, loved ones, and a sane outlook on life? Do you long to become a bitter and friendless curmudgeon?

Then welcome to this chapter's lesson, a miniseminar titled (appropriately) "How to Become a Bitter and Friendless Curmudgeon." Here you'll learn how to identify and seize upon opportunities to cling to bogus language "rules" as if they were your only friends. Indeed, with any luck, they soon will be. And, best of all, you can achieve this lifelong dream with just three easy steps.

Step 1: Read the first definition for any word in the dictionary.

Step 2: Stop there, refusing to read any subsequent definitions.

Step 3: Hurl cheap insults at anyone who accepts any definition other than yours.

Start with the A's—specifically, with "aggravate."

"Aggravate" is one of the most ire-raising words in the usage guides. Most experts caution against using it as a synonym for "irritate" or "annoy," usually in pretty cranky terms. But only a rare few go the extra mile required to qualify themselves as bona fide bitter and friendless curmudgeons by skipping mere warnings to opt instead for flat-out prohibitions—prohibitions based on nothing more than their own preferences. These style freaks are role models in your quest for a life of surly solitude.

Take Strunk and White: "'Aggravate.' 'Irritate.' The first means 'to add to' an already troublesome or vexing matter or condition. The second means 'to vex' or 'to annoy' or 'to chafe.'"

Anyone who wants to subscribe to this black-and-white view of the words should be sure to read *Webster's New World College Dictionary*'s first entry for "aggravate": "1. to make worse; make more burdensome, troublesome, etc." But they should stop reading there; otherwise they would see this second entry: "2. [Informal] to exasperate; annoy; vex."

"Aggravate" originally meant to exacerbate or to make worse or add to. But it's been used as a synonym for "irritate" for at least four centuries—long enough and widely enough that dictionaries have had no choice but to acknowledge it. But the style boss men don't like it in the least. Even as they grudgingly accept that this secondary definition of "aggravate" is permissible, most can't resist getting a few shots in.

"Aggravate: Commonly, but not by a careful writer, this word is used to mean irritate. Neither the commonness nor the long history of the misuse makes it any better than inept," Theodore Bernstein tells us in *The Careful Writer*.

"Avoid 'aggravate' in the sense 'to annoy, to exasperate, to provoke'; but humdrum writers and hurried journalists may, if they wish, take heart of disgrace from the fact that 'aggravate' has been used in these nuances since early in the 17th century," Eric Partridge tells us in *Usage and Abusage*. "But pedants must cease from stigmatizing the word as bad English; it can no longer be classified as anything worse than an infelicity."

If you're looking for a calmly worded, middle-of-the-road answer, consider jumping on board with *Garner's:* "'Aggravate' for 'annoy' or 'irritate' has never gained the approval of stylists and should be avoided in formal writing."

But if you're truly on the path to a curmudgeonly destiny, you'll settle for nothing less than a flat-out, foaming-at-the-mouth, absolute prohibition that will no doubt inspire people to think of you as "extremely aggravating."

The tyrant <u>lobbed</u> off their heads.

This usage is: A clear mistake, utterly mortifying to a person who made it and who shall here remain unnamed.

A certain unnamed person, while writing a certain entertaining and informative column, once used the word "lobbed" when she—er, uh, she *or he*—meant "lopped." A reader, whose e-mail has since mysteriously disappeared, pointed out the error.

To "lob," *Webster's New World College Dictionary* tells us, is "1. to move heavily and clumsily," or "2. to lob a ball." On the other hand, *Webster's* says "lop. vt. 1. to trim (a tree, etc.) by cutting off branches, twigs, or stems. 2. to remove by or as by cutting off: usually with 'off.'"

The bad news is that the person who made this mistake got in trouble for it. The good news is that she now better understands one particular *Seinfeld* episode. In it, Jerry, who has just broken up with his girlfriend, is afraid to leave her apartment because there's a serial killer in the neighborhood. Finally, I—I mean, the person in question—understand that the killer was "The Lopper," as in "lops off heads," and not The Lauper, as in Cyndi. Now if only someone could explain to me the lyrics of Cyndi's song "She Lop."

There's taxes to pay.

This usage is: Icky.

*I*n the days leading up to the American Revolution, a common cry of the colonists was "no taxation without representation." Even a history-impaired person like me can understand this (although certain questions remain, such as why didn't they do something more effective than just throw a tea party or at least switch to a more American drink like lattes or Red Bull).

I bring this up now not to show off my vast knowledge of U.S. history but because the double standard of taxation without representation reminds me of my single biggest grammar beef: We're all expected to know stuff we were probably never taught. Then we're picked on for not knowing it. It's vexation without education.

For example, a lot of us cringe when we hear "there's" followed by a plural. "There's many things to drink besides tea." "There's some people in red coats I want you to meet." "There's eight of us who still haven't signed this document but John Hancock is hogging up half the page."

All these "there's" should be "there are," right?

Right?

There *are* many things. There *are* some people. There *are* eight of us.

Yeah. Sure. But here's the rub: Why?

"There's," as we know, is a contraction of "there" and "is." So anybody who cringes when he hears "There's men here," no doubt also knows that verbs should agree with their subjects. But if you ask that same person why the verb is plural to agree with "men" instead of singular to agree with "there," chances are he'll turn tail like a redcoat in the streets of wherever it was the redcoats were coming from.

Isn't "there" in the subject position in both "There *is* a man" and "There *are* some men"? Why does the verb seem to agree not with the subject of the sentence but with the complement of the verb?

Enter a term your English teacher probably never taught you (possibly because she'd never heard it herself): "notional subject."

A rather disturbing discussion of all this stuff can be found in *The Oxford English Grammar* under the heading of another term your English teacher probably never taught you: the "existential *there.*"

That's the term *Oxford* uses to describe this "there." And though it may function grammatically as the subject of a sentence, it's really just booting the true subject—the notional subject—down to a lower status. "There are men here" is just a flip-flopped way of saying, "Men are here." So while "there" functions as the "grammatical subject," in *Oxford*-speak, "men" is the notional subject.

Putting things back in terms of our history lesson, "There are wine coolers in Jefferson's minifridge" is just a flip-flopped way of saying, "Wine coolers are in Jefferson's minifridge." In both cases, the "there" is just an extra word we throw in to help us control the emphasis.

In that last example, "wine coolers" is the true subject being discussed. It just happens to be relegated to a different grammatical position by the bullying existential "there."

So grammarians use the term "notional subject" to help us understand this situation. And from here we find the roots of our long-held but never explained instinct that the notional subject determines the verb conjugation.

There *are* many reasons for men to wear stockings. There *is* a good reason for men to wear stockings: There *is* nothing better than this silky feeling against a man's skin.

Using the term "inverted verb," *Garner's* backs up the logic we were unable to articulate all along: "*There is; there are.* . . . The number of the verb is controlled by whether the subject that follows the inverted verb is singular or plural."

Fowler's agrees.

If it were up to me, the discussion would end here. Unfortunately, I found this nasty little twist in *Oxford:* "Like other grammatical subjects, [existential 'there'] often determines the number concord, taking a singular verb even though the notional subject is plural. This usage is common in informal speech."

Note that "informal."

Oxford gives examples: "There was elements of it that were fun." "There's no seats left on that day."

In writing this book, my policy is to never tell you that you can't do something that an established grammar authority tells you is okay. I'm just not qualified to contradict *Oxford.* So I'd be overstepping my bounds if I said you can't write "There's many people." But here's what I can, in good conscience, say about such constructions: Yuck.

Fowler's shares my disdain, saying it is "uneducated speech."

So if you want to sound good to language book authors and history experts, avoid "there's" with a plural subject (that is, a plural notional subject). But if you like pushing the rules to their limits, if you're a rebel who questions everything up to and including whether we were wise to trade in the king's rule for today's Congress, use "there's" whenever you like.

41

Infighting among experts is a <u>reoccurring</u> phenomenon.

This usage is: Probably not wise.

*R*ight about now, you're probably thinking: June, I know grammar is hilarious and all, a thrill ride of cosmic proportions that's like a bungee jump, a tequila shooter, and a Rita Rudner show all rolled up into one, but sometimes I'd rather watch mold grow or listen to my grandmother discuss the latest developments in her bursitis. What do you recommend?

My answer: How about reading a bit about the spine-tingling debate over "recur" and "reoccur"?

Start by seeking out the advice of those who would clobber you for using "reoccur," like the guy named Henry who posted this on the Music Player Network Expert Forums: "Another [word I hate] is 'reoccur.' It's 'recur.' Drives me batty."

Then, for even more thrills, see what the experts have to say on the subject. Excitingly, the experts disagree on "reoccur." Some say it's a legitimate word subtly different from "recur." Others say it's just a poor substitute.

Bernstein and Garner are its two biggest defenders:

"'Reoccur' suggests a one-time repetition. 'Recur' suggests a repetition more than once, usually according to some fixed schedule, as in 'the recurring phases of the moon,'" Bernstein argues in *The Careful Writer*.

I would add that if prefixes allow you to make a new compound out of any word, there's no reason you can't slap a "re" onto "occur" in situations where the existing word "recur" doesn't cut it.

Opponents of "reoccur" include *AP*, which says to use "recur" instead, and Fiske, who says, "Neither 'reoccur' nor 'reoccurrence' should exist in any reputable English-language lexicon."

But perhaps the most poignant commentary on "reoccur" isn't what's said about this word. It's what is not said. *Webster's New World College Dictionary* doesn't mention "reoccur," not even to dis it. Neither does *The American Heritage Dictionary*.

And that's about all the thrills I can handle on this one.

42

Aren't I right to use this contraction?

This usage is: Rock-freakin'-solid.

*T*oday (well, my today; your ten to fourteen months ago) I checked my e-mail and found three—count 'em, three—e-mails from readers of my column telling me I was wrong to write "aren't I."

Here's what I had written: "Aren't I just discriminating against people who hate grammar?"

Here's how one of them responded: "Who's proofreading your [*Burbank*] *Leader* grammar column? . . . Did you mean *am I not* instead of *aren't I*? Perhaps this was mean to be a humoprous error." (Yup. He wrote "humoprous." Yup, he wrote "mean." I know, I know.)

Here's how another responded: "The use of *aren't* is very common but actually incorrect in the above quote. Unfortunately, the alternative is a rather stuffy-uppity-sounding *am I not.*"

Here's how the smartest of the three responded: "In today's article—paragraph 2, sentence 2, *aren't' I?*—I might have said, *am I not?* That's a single subject witha single verb. Perhaps there a special rule. . . . Please advise." (Yup: "witha." Yup: "there a special rule." I feel a little guilty for not fixing these readers' typos, as I customarily do before I reprint stuff. But in context, these are just too humoprous.)

Fun with typos aside, what we have here are three people who looked at the words "aren't I" and decided, all by themselves, that this must be wrong. Since it's "I am" instead of "I are," then surely "are" has no business pairing up with "I" in "aren't I," they reasoned.

There's just one little problem with this logic: These people, like you and me, have been hearing "aren't I" their entire lives. They know perfectly well that it's common, standard even. Therefore, they're questioning—two of them refuting—a standard usage *without bothering to look it up.*

"Rules" in any arena are seldom universal. The people who wrote these e-mails know perfectly well that the constitutional right to free speech doesn't cover everything you might say to an airline pilot or a congressional page or members of an audience who loved you on *Seinfeld* and assume you can do stand-up.

So these people should have considered the possibility that maybe—just maybe—the overwhelming popularity of "aren't I" over "am I not" and the shortened "amn't I" means it's sanctioned by the grammar gods.

Of course it is.

"*Aren't I,* though illogical, is the standard contraction corresponding to *am I not,*" writes Bryan Garner in *Garner's Modern American Usage,* adding that "amn't" is "dialectical and substandard."

The Oxford English Grammar agrees, as do H. W. Fowler and Eric Partridge. None of my sources disagree.

Perhaps I'm being a little too rough on the three people who e-mailed me. But, as Bugs Bunny might say, am I not a stinker?

43

You have <u>woken up</u> the beast.

This usage is: Risky business.

*D*ear reader: I write you this letter at great peril and fearing for my own life, as I am about to expose the secret doings of a great power monitoring our very speech.

I'm speaking, of course, of linguists—academics who position themselves as liberal freedom fighters against the oppressive "prescriptivists" in our current language wars but who themselves sometimes employ devious tactics including, it's true, surveillance.

I myself have been attacked by these "descriptivist" forces and have barely lived to tell. So you see why it is only at great peril that I expose their dark secrets. The truth must be told.

First, you must know that the most powerful weapons these linguists wield are sketchy at best and ill-gotten at worst. They're called "corpora," plural for "corpus," and they are often multimillion-word collections of English usage gathered not just from printed sources but from public and private speech as well. That's right; "information gatherers" running around with tape recorders documenting their every conversation* have added to

---

* From what I can tell, most or all corpora projects that include spoken English didn't obtain the examples as underhandedly as I make it sound. Some, if not all, required their word gatherers to get permission from all the speakers they recorded. But this fact, while offering a better picture of what's really going on, would have sucked the drama right out of my story.

these corpora. And what linguists do with these documents is just as shocking.

Whenever someone touts an English rule that some linguist disagrees with, the linguist just searches these corpora for examples of people breaking the rule. And voilà, that's their proof that no such rule exists.

My brush with these dangerous forces is a case in point. Some time back, I wrote a column explaining Bryan Garner's rules on forming past tenses of "wake," "wake up," "awake," and "awaken."

The past tense and past participle of "wake," he wrote and I reported, are "woke" and "waked" (or "woken"). The past tense and participle of "awake" are "awoke" and "awaked" (or "awoken"). The past tense and past participle of "awaken" are both "awakened." And the past forms of "wake up" are "woke up" and "waked up."

In summing up, I chose my words poorly. "There is no 'woken up,' " I wrote.

Then I found it. My name, my words, broadcast on a blog of the enemy—I had been identified and blacklisted.

There was a "woken up," the linguist blogger insisted, and he could prove it.

This leads us to the second terrifying truth about linguists—a new development in their horrifying tactics: They no longer even need corpora. They can just Google instead.

And Google he did, culling many examples of "woken up" used at sites such as (I'm just guessing here) "Kaitlin's Awesome Weekend at Camp" and "Captain Conservative's Wake-Up Call for Wimpy Liberals."

And if Kaitlin and Captain Conservative use "woken up," who am I to use *Garner's* as a source for a column?

Now you know their secret. You see their tactics. So go, and tell the world before it's too late. Godspeed.

44

**Instead of studying hard,
I just <u>perused</u> my textbook.**

This usage is: Bad.

𝓕or all who dream of a career in the exciting world of community newspaper editing, here's a little quiz to see if you've got what it takes. Read the following excerpt from a newspaper humor column and ask yourself: If I could change anything at all in this excerpt, what would it be?

> My last apartment offered a potpourri of neighbor smells including burnt toast, marijuana smoke and spices that must have been smuggled into the country in dress shields. So I began to develop the habit of casually perusing the rentals section of the classifieds— looking for headlines like "Odor-free living at its best!"

Now, if your answer is that you would change the word "perusing" to "skimming," I'm afraid you don't have the chops for community newspaper editing. You see, that would reflect an expert understanding of English usage, and such knowledge is intolerable at certain papers that shall remain nameless.

No, the answer you should have given is that you would change "spices that must have been smuggled into the country in dress shields" to "spices that must have been smuggled into the country while sewn into women's clothing."

That's because, as certain community news editors demonstrate, their job is not to catch real errors but to squash the humor and creativity out of every piece of writing that comes across their desks, replacing jokes they don't like with verbose, diluted wordings that make no sense. If a reporter writing a humor column about New Year's resolutions jokes about learning to play the lute, change it to "flute." If she writes, "Here are three titles of upcoming books," and you don't like one because it mocks SUV drivers, just take that one out. But be sure to leave the "Here are three" to introduce what are now two.

Okay, maybe I'm being a little unfair to the editors here. In my first example, the "peruse" part of that quote didn't really appear. I added it here in order to make a lesson out of what would otherwise be just a passive-aggressive rant about frustrated editors stuck in low-paying, dead-end jobs that seem to mock their *New York Times* dreams, and who therefore derive pleasure from inflicting harm on other people's prose. Because, you see, all of those other editor "improvements" really happened— the "lute" changed to "flute," the edited-in counting error, and, most bafflingly, the one about "while sewn into women's clothing."

Yup, some editor somewhere thought that was a perfectly peachy alternative to "in dress shields"—as if women's clothing were synonymous with stench (raising serious questions about the hygiene of the editor's female relations that I, for one, am far too noble to point out here even though I just did).

A fact little known to the people who like to mess up others' writing: "Peruse," in its purest form, doesn't mean to skim casually. It means to scrutinize, to study carefully—the exact opposite of the way most people use it today.

And, of course, whenever most people start using a word "wrong," it ends up being right. That's why many dictionaries now include this more recent definition of "peruse." But *The American Heritage Dictionary*, even as it offers this option, goes on to explain the sentiments of its panel of wordsmith experts regarding the word "peruse":

> Some people use it to mean *to glance over, skim*, as in "I only had a moment to peruse the manual quickly," but this usage is widely considered an error. In a 1988 survey, 66 percent of the panel found it unacceptable and in 1999, 58 percent still rejected it.

What this means to you is that if you're ever trusted with the responsibility of ensuring the quality of someone else's writing, you should help that writer best use "peruse" instead of obliterating a perfectly good reference to dress shields.

45

**<u>Bring</u> this hood-mounted ray
gun on your morning commute.**

This usage is: Very tricky.

*A*s a change of pace from the glamorous life of an author,
sometimes I shed my bunny slippers to do freelance proofreading
work at a big-time ad agency. I don't want to name names, but if
you ever see a magazine spread for a midsize luxury car that gets
25 mpg city, 300 highway, you'll recognize my handiwork. (Well,
mine or Ed Begley Jr.'s.)

While the upside of this gig is that they keep hiring me no
matter how inadequate or actionable my work, the downside is
that it's in Santa Monica, thirty-odd miles away from my house
in Pasadena. Now, I know what all of you in Wyoming and Mon-
tana are thinking: How horrible! A thirty-minute commute!

Yeah, right.

In the morning I allow an hour and forty-five minutes, which
usually gets me there two to four minutes prior to my bladder
bursting.

Getting home is even more fun. On what I have since declared
to be my last day at the agency—a day radio announcers noted
there was "very heavy" traffic but no accidents or problems any-
where on my route—it took me two and a half hours to get home.
Fifty-five minutes of that was spent traversing three blocks to the
freeway on-ramp. No kidding. Fifty-five infuriating, homicidal,
"wait-till-I-get-my-hands-on-the-city-officials-who-approved-a-

massive-office-complex-on-a-narrow-and-already-congested-road" minutes. Obviously, I've had a lot of time to think about traffic solutions. And I have some good ones. But as we well know, most solutions to our nation's traffic problems have a common flaw. They all cost money.

But I think I've found a way to finance every one of my costly traffic fixes—from double-deckering the freeways to sexual favors for motorcyclists to "Rolex Day" on the Metro bus. Here it is: Tax all the automotive luxuries that have proven themselves to be, for some, completely inelastic commodities.

For example, any adhesive sticker that reports what the driver would rather be doing—well, let's slap about $500 on those. Trust me, the windsurfers and Jazzercizers will cough it up. And how much will parents pay to keep the kids' eyes glued to that onboard DVD player? I'm guessing they'd pay up to and including $1,500 a year in the form of a "mobile *Finding Nemo* child-sedation fee." And have you ever seen a Mini-Cooper driver who wouldn't pay hundreds to work the word "Mini" into a vanity license plate? Every time Calvin pees on anyone or anything there should be an $800 charge. When he prays, let's make it $900.

As you can see, helpful advice is my forte. Unfortunately, grammar is the only subject on which I can reach an audience (curse those fast-moving bodyguards at the governor's mansion).

So until the publication of my upcoming book, *Elected Officials Who Don't Make Me Traffic Czar Are Great Big Meanies*, I'll stick to language topics.

Take "bring" (please).

"Bring" suggests movement toward the speaker or writer: "Bring me a hood-mounted grenade launcher." "Bring me some Xanax." "Bring me a higher-functioning state government."

"Take" suggests movement away from the speaker or writer: "Take this hood-mounted grenade launcher with you." "Take a bottle of Xanax in the car with you." "Take my governor, please."

In those examples, the difference is clear. And according to some books, including *Chicago, The Dictionary of Disagreeable English*, and *Usage and Abusage*, that's all you need to know.

Unfortunately, it's not that simple.

"There are many circumstances, however, in which this simple distinction does not apply," *Fowler's* tells us.

For example, what happens when the movement really doesn't have anything to do with the location of the speaker or writer, as in this *Garner's* example: "My father used to take bags of groceries to my mother."

And what happens when the speaker or writer is moving right along with the thing being brought or taken, as in this *Fowler's* example: "If we are going to the zoo shall we bring/take the camera?"

Suddenly, the experts start to sound a lot less confident—and a lot less useful. For example, *Fowler's* uses the zoo example to demonstrate a perplexing question that it never bothers to answer. The authors just leave us hanging.

For the *Garner's* example, the author suggests that the choice between "bring" and "take" "depends on the motion toward or away from whatever is being discussed." So, he says, the grocery bag example could use "take" or "bring," depending on whether it's from the mother's point of view or the father's.

That's when the supposedly simple rule of "bring" and "take" can become subject to your own judgment call. And it's also when experts like Eric Partridge, who wrote, "'Bring' is confused with 'take' only by the illiterate or unthinking," can be every bit as infuriating as a two-and-half-hour commute.

46

Johnny Damon shouldn't have <u>went</u> to New York.

This usage is: Ungrammatical.

*I*f you believe that Johnny Damon shouldn't have *went* to New York, if you like to speculate about whether the Patriots should have *beat* the Colts, if sometimes after a meal you bonk your head and say, "I could have *ate* some beans," you're probably from the Boston area. You may also be sports-obsessed, gassy, and ungrammatical, but I can only help you with the grammar.

There are linguists, lexicographers, and usage experts who would defend constructions such as "he should have went" as regional colloquialisms. But if you or someone you love (shout out to my Walpole, Mass., homeys) talks like this, remember: Before you break the rules, make sure you've got them down pat. Because this is one language crime the grammar cops won't tolerate.

"I cringe a lot when I hear people talk—not just kids! Like I HAVE WENT . . . or HE HAS TOOK," notes a user at the Ask Grandma T blog. "Oooohhh . . . like fingernails on chalk board to my ears!!"

Here's the rule you should know to avoid their wrath.

Take a sentence like "I have realized the dangers of bean eating." Here, the verb "realized" is conjugated in what most call the "present perfect" tense (rather annoying that it's called "present" even though it's clearly past. But if your English teacher skipped this stuff entirely, at least now you know why).

Anyway, this tense is created by adding a form of present tense "have" to a "past participle" (what some others call a "perfect participle") such as "walked," "heard," "eaten," "risen," or "thought."

With many verbs, the participle is identical to the simple past tense:

> I walked. I have walked.
> He thought. He has thought.
> They worked. They have worked.

But there are also "irregular verbs"—words you use all the time probably without even noticing the difference:

> I rose. I have risen.
> He chose. He has chosen.
> They did it. They have done it.

As I said, this is pretty intuitive stuff for most of us, except the rare breed I hereby dub the Boston Mangler.

The Mangler has no use for irregular participles. The simple past-tense forms are enough for him.

He changes the correct "I should have *gone*" to the incorrect "I should have *went*." "They should have *beaten*" in his hands becomes "They should have *beat*." And the correct "I should have *eaten*" gets mangled into "I should have *ate*."

But you need not fall victim to this habit. Take note of the common irregular participles shown in the table. These, not their simple past-tense cousins, are the ones to follow "have," "has," and "had." When in doubt, just check your dictionary, which lists irregular forms under each main word. So right under "eat" you'll see the simple past tense "ate," followed by the participle "eaten."

Common Irregular Participles

arisen	fallen	swollen
beaten	mown	sworn
become	ridden	swum
begun	rung	taken
blown	seen	thrown
broken	sewn	torn
chosen	shrunk	woken
drawn	slain	worn
driven	spoken	written
drunk	stolen	
eaten	sung	

In other words, once you have driven (not drove) to the ballpark and you have eaten (not ate) a Fenway Frank, only then will you have shaken (not shook) the curse of the Boston Mangler.

47

Bob likes to <u>patronize</u> minority-owned businesses.

This usage is: Okay, but you can do better.

*O*n an episode of *Cheers*, resident smarty-pants Frasier Crane offered advice to a fellow barfly on the word "patronize." Unfortunately, I saw this episode ages ago, long before I developed my obsessive habit of scribbling notes about any potential grammar book fodder I hear on TV. (Yes, dear reader, I vigilantly take notes while watching TV. That's the level of service and dedication I bring to you, except when a cat is on my lap. They don't like to be disturbed.)

So I can't promise you I'm getting Frasier's wording exactly right, but as I remember it, he corrected someone else for talking about "patronizing" a business. The correct usage, he said, would be something like "Thank you for your patronage." He pronounced the first syllable with a short "a" as in Pat instead of with a long "a" as in Kate.

Ever since, I've been completely insecure in my use of "patronize." Does it mean to support someone or to dis him? I spent countless hours over many years trying to find a clear answer, but my efforts were in vain: No other TV show would explain it to me. (Thanks a lot, Dave Chappelle.)

Finally, in last-ditch desperation, I opened a dictionary: "Patronize: 1. to act as a patron toward; sponsor; support; 2. to be kind or helpful to, but in a haughty or snobbish way, as if dealing with an inferior."

In other words, you can patronize a restaurant by eating there, or you can patronize its owner by carefully explaining to him why the day-old oyster sushi special isn't a hit.

The dictionary also solved my pronunciation confusion. Both pronunciations are correct, but the first choice of *Webster's* is the long "a," as in Kate.

The style and usage guides don't have much to say on the matter. I guess they figure most people are smart enough to just open the dictionary. Their only bits of advice on "patron" and "patronize" suggest that these words, in business applications, are a bunch of hot air: "*Patron* for *customer* is a piece of commercial ostentation," *The Careful Writer* opines; "*Patronize* for *trade with* . . . is commercial pretentiousness," *Usage and Abusage* advises, adding: "Patron of the arts, but not of a green-grocer or a bookmaker."

After learning all this, I confess I feel a little betrayed by our nation's most trusted source of information, prime-time TV. In retrospect, I guess I should have been more hesitant to accept language advice delivered by an actor who spells his last name Grammer.

48

What it <u>is is</u> people don't like these constructions.

This usage is: Grammatical yet goofy.

$\mathcal{T}$here's only one reason you're reading this chapter: You want to use "is is." Perhaps you're the type of person who'd like to brazenly needle the usage mavens of the world by saying stuff like "What it is is you're wrong." Or perhaps you're fending off Ken Starr. Either way, unlike all the people in the world who are perfectly content just avoiding this construction—the people who flipped right past this chapter to a more useful rant about "enormity"—you want to push the limits.

Good for you.

Here's what you need to know. Yes, "what it is is" is widely frowned upon and considered awkward (rightly so). But that doesn't mean it's ungrammatical. In this construction, "what it is" is functioning as a single unit—the subject of the sentence. And subjects require verbs, hence that second "is." This is also why most authorities say you shouldn't put a comma between the ises. To do so would be the equivalent of separating a subject from its verb, like "The cat, is black."

The main authority that disagrees is *AP*. In its punctuation section, *AP* advises: "Use a comma to separate duplicated words that otherwise would be confusing: *What the problem is, is not clear.*"

But, *AP* or no *AP*, remember that the standard rules of commas apply, such as the comma after the introductory clause in Bill

Walsh's example (in *Lapsing into a Comma*): "The question is, is history going to look kindly on the Clinton presidency?" In this case, the first "is" ends an introductory clause, which would have a comma regardless of whether it creates a double "is." For comparison, consider "The question is, will history . . ." And because that would take a comma, Walsh's example takes a comma, too.

But if you want to use "is is," brace yourself for a fight. People call this construction "ungainly," "weird," and other not-very-nice things.

Also, take note that not every "is is" is grammatical. It has become a pretty common thing in speech to say stuff like "The problem is is . . ." The problem is that this is a different case entirely. Unlike "what it is," the subject "the problem" doesn't include an "is," making the second one totally redundant. It's like saying "The cat is is black."

So go forth now, into the world, and pick your "is is" battles carefully—but with confidence.

PART IV

Noun Sequitur

49

The <u>enormity</u> of the Grand Canyon is overwhelming.

This usage is: Enormously frowned upon.

*F*irst, here's what you need to know about "enormity": Size doesn't matter. I know it seems as if "enormity" is just a noun form of the adjective "enormous," but that's not how the bosses see it.

"These days, educated writers and speakers reserve 'enormity' for the meaning 'great evil or wickedness,'" writes Bill Walsh in *Lapsing into a Comma.*

All nine of my style books that mention "enormity"—from Strunk and White's to *Fowler's* to *Garner's* and Bernstein—agree this word is not about bigness, it's about badness. For bigness, they say, use "enormousness" or "hugeness" or maybe "magnitude."

But the style gurus' discussion of this word reveals a little more than they want it to. Perhaps more than for any other word I researched for this book, the experts' opinions are tinged with editorializing and moralizing and the very revealing word "should."

Take Walsh's next sentence: "I think this distinction should be observed."

And Garner: "The historical differentiation between these words should not be muddled."

And Fiske: "Enough of this misusage. *Enormity* is a word like no other; let us not disembowel it by using it as a synonym for *enormousness.*"

And the topper, from Wallraff: "If we are moral people, we should strive to retain *enormity* as one of the few words adequate to decry historic events on the scale of the Serbian slaughter of Albanians in Kosovo in 1999, the mid-1990s genocide in Rwanda, and Hitler's Holocaust."

That's an awfully tall order for one easily confused little word.

And the dictionary, even as it documents deviations, can't do so without a tinge of judgment, though attributed to others. Says *Webster's* third entry for "enormity": "enormous size or extent; vastness: in modern use, considered a loose usage by some."

Of course, in the academic world you'll find some leeway: "The [*Oxford English Dictionary*] agrees that the use of enormity to mean *bigness* . . . is obsolete, and its citations for that sense are all from the late 18th or early 19th century," writes linguist Mark Liberman. "But if *enormity* could mean *enormousness* in 1830, who's to say that we have to hold the line 'until the end of time' against the return of that sense?"

Considering the surprised faces I've encountered when, during public talks, I explained the meaning of "enormity," my prediction is that "enormity" is doomed to once again mean "enormousness."

But it's not there yet. So use it accordingly.

50

This term creates <u>a myriad of</u> problems.

This usage is: As valid as "myriad problems" but not as well liked.

*O*nce upon a time, I single-handedly saved the city of Newport Beach.

It was the day of the big Mayor's Dinner—an annual event that has attracted the likes of then-congressman Christopher Cox (who one year drew a comedic comparison between the mayors of his two hometowns: Newport Beach and Washington, D.C. Cox's tales of the wacky antics of crackhead Marion Barry turned the overwhelmingly white crowd overwhelmingly pink).

I was a city hall reporter covering Newport Beach for a small newspaper full of Botox ads. My job was to cover the mayor's speech, then file a story for the next day's paper. The problem was that the speech was at nine o'clock and the paper's deadline was nine thirty (or something like that).

Here's where I let you in on a little reporters' secret. Often, when covering an event that runs late, a reporter will write the story in advance, based on what she thinks is going to happen. Then she'll call her editor from the event to say, "Run it as-is," or, "Add this quote about Marion Barry's hair on fire." When a reporter can't make a good guess about an outcome—say, for example, a city council vote—she might even file two stories with opposite outcomes, calling in later to tell the editors which one to run. Risky as it sounds, it's a system that actually works—for some things.

A speech is different, of course. You can't know what the official is going to say. Right?

Wrong.

Here's another little reporters' secret. All you do is call the mayor at 4 P.M. and ask him to fax you a copy of the speech he'll give. Assuming he's not a crackhead, he should be able to locate a copy.

So on the night of the big Newport Beach Mayor's Dinner, I asked the mayor to fax me his speech. He did, and that's when I saw it—a catastrophe in the making, a bumble so bumbling that it could have cost the mayor his credibility, rocking Newport Beach to its Gucci loafers: the words "a myriad of."

I called the mayor.

"Good speech," I said, pretending to be a great admirer of oration on the subject of zoning restrictions and parking meter revenues. "Just one little thing. You might want to change 'a myriad of' to just 'myriad.'"

I then showered him with my wisdom: It's not "a myriad of issues." It's "myriad issues." It's not "a myriad of problems." It's "myriad problems."

Thanking me with all the sincerity of a congressional page receiving a warning about an overfriendly congressman, the mayor made the change.

The speech was a rousing success. I felt a gush of personal pride when he spoke with well-chosen words about "myriad issues." And the city was saved from catastrophe.

There was just one problem. I was wrong.

I have no idea where I got that bit of bad information. It's not documented in any of my style guides. But I'm not the first to botch this. A reader of Barbara Wallraff's language column in the *Atlantic Monthly* wrote that she once got a lower grade on a paper because, the teacher said, she used "myriad" instead of "a myriad of." Same confusion, just backwards.

Here's the real deal on "myriad." Both ways are fine. It is both an adjective ("myriad problems"), and a noun ("a myriad of problems"). Both Garner and Walsh prefer the adjective, but none of my sources will tell you that either is wrong.

You might care to know that "myriad" comes from the Greek word for ten thousand, and it retained that meaning in English up until a century or two ago. Then again, you might not. Now it just means a great many—like the number of thanks that Newport Beach owes to me for sharing my great wisdom, and that Christopher Cox (now chairman of the Securities and Exchange Commission) owes me for not printing any of his Marion Barry jokes.

51

What's the dog's <u>gender</u>?

This usage is: Controversial but acceptable.

Speaking of subjects on which I'm completely unqualified to dispense advice but do so anyway, I'd like to talk about sex.

Sex is something I had to learn about the hard way—not just in the streets but in public, in front of thousands of scrutinizing eyes.

What? No! Not like that! I'm talking about the correct usage of the word "sex" and its partner, "gender."

Of course, grammar is a lot like sex. If you're lucky, you'll make it through your entire life without someone pointing out everything you're doing wrong. I wasn't so lucky. In the early days of my grammar column, I told readers that the word "gender" should not be used to mean "sex."

"There are separate locker rooms for each gender" is a usage I then labeled wrong. I was unaware, at the time, that not everyone swings the same way on this subject.

For example, Bernstein's *The Careful Writer*, which was written in 1965 and whose huge influence continues today, says, "Gender is a grammatical term. . . . It is not a substitute for sex (but, then, what is?)."

Cute, yes, but is this right? Well, somehow the author managed to overlook or ignore one of the most important works to precede him, *Usage and Abusage*, which in 1942 said that the use of "gender" for "sex" is "rapidly becoming a vogue word."

And with the words "rapidly becoming," this author some-how managed to overlook or ignore a little book called *The Oxford English Dictionary*, which cites "gender" being used as "sex" as far back as 1709.

Feminism has further complicated the matter. At one point some feminists started using the word "gender" to emphasize the cultural differences between men and women, reserving the word "sex" to refer to biological differences. And there's hardly a writer under the sun who will pass up an opportunity to take a shot at feminists and/or the political correctness so closely associated with them:

"The ['gender equity'] industry prefers the word 'gender' to 'sex,'" George Will has written.

"People who contend that no sexual behavior should be con-sidered unusual have adopted the word to express such thoughts as 'Johnny is a member of the male sex, but he likes to wear dresses, so he's of the female gender,'" Bill Walsh has opined.

From these two excerpts alone, you'd suspect that any day now a massive gender-equity "industry" and the enormous "no-sex-is-abnormal" crowd could soon overrun the beloved tradi-tional values still preserved in the form of 50 Cent videos and vintage Andrew Dice Clay HBO specials.

But I digress.

Back on topic, when it comes to sex and gender, remember that traditionalists say that "sex" is the best word to describe the physical difference between boys and girls. "Gender," they say, re-fers to things like pronouns in English and nouns and pronouns in a lot of other languages—think "*la revolución*" (feminine) versus "*el jefe*" (masculine). But if you feel like burning the theoretical brassiere of tradition, know that *Fowler's, Garner's, Usage and Abu-sage*, Barbara Wallraff, Bill Walsh, and, most important of all, *Webster's* all support sometimes using "gender" to mean the physi-cal difference between men and women.

52

**A <u>majority</u> of the human race
have better things to worry about.**

This usage is: Frowned upon.

*J*ust when I thought I'd heard it all, I learned that there are people out there who have the time and energy to get annoyed at others' use of the word "majority."

"One of my pet peeves (is) the overuse and, I think, misuse of 'majority' instead of 'most,'" a reader named Nancy wrote to me. "For example, 'He spends a marjority [*sic*] of him [*sic*] time on the telephone.' Is this usage incorrect or just annoying?" (Answer: Not as annoying as reading a rant like this that's loaded with typos.)

Luckily, these people seem to be a minority.

"Majority," they say, should not apply to noncountable things, like time or news. In fact, they say, you should never use "majority" where "most" would do.

Yes, while the rest of the nation still marvels at the fact that the majority doesn't always get to pick our president, other people are nitpicking the word in far less meaningful contexts.

Are they right? That depends on who you trust, which in turn is probably related to whether you'd change that to "whom you trust."

Bryan Garner, H. W. Fowler, and Eric Partridge are the only authorities in my library who take a position on "majority." And they all think its use should be restricted.

In *Fowler's* view, it depends on what comes afterward: "*The majority of* cannot properly be followed by an uncountable noun," *Fowler's Modern English Usage* tells us. "Thus, *a* (or *the*) *majority of experience, forgiveness, interest, tolerance, work,* etc., are all unidiomatic."

So, according to *Fowler's*, you can have a majority of votes or a majority of Supreme Court justices in your pocket because these are all individually counted things. But you can't have a majority of the support.

Partridge agrees, saying that "majority" cannot mean "a larger part" of something, such as a book. So according to them, "The majority of the book was interesting" and "The majority of history is written by the winners" are wrong.

Garner doesn't go so far as to lay down absolute right and wrong, but he's basically on the same team: "When *most* will suffice, use it in place of *majority.*"

Webster's leaves a lot more elbow room: "majority . . . the greater part."

On the question of whether "majority" takes a singular or plural verb, again, there's some flexibility. When you're using "majority" to emphasize multiple things, a plural verb is fine: "When it comes to voters, the majority *want* their votes to count." When you're talking about a majority as a unit, a single verb is fine. "The majority *rules*—supposedly."

53

Have a seat on this lovely chaise <u>lounge</u>.

This usage is: Wrong according to most, "folk etymology" according to some.

Maybe we should be a little more forgiving of "chaise *lounge*." After all, in a country where Congress once insisted on scarfing only "freedom fries" and where a former presidential candidate was actually ridiculed for speaking French, can we really blame people for not knowing it's the straight-from-the-French "chaise *longue*"?

The books in my arsenal that discuss this are *Garner's, Lapsing Into a Comma, The Dictionary of Disagreeable English, Fowler's, Webster's,* and *The American Heritage Dictionary.* They stand united, giving nary a tip of the beret to "lounge." It's the wrong word, they say. You want "longue"—French for "long."

"Some people commit the embarrassing error of saying or writing *chaise lounge.* . . . The problem is that *lounge,* when put after *chaise,* looks distinctly low-rent," says *Garner's.*

By the way, it's pronounced "shayz long" according to *Garner's,* "shez long" according to my own horrible French, and it means literally "long chair" or "couchlike chair." The plural used to be "chaises longues," in keeping with the traditional French way of forming plurals. But now most chaise-savvy Americans are just writing "chaise longues."

Either way, they're great to sit on while eating freedom fries.

54

Under the <u>pretense</u> of being helpful, *AP* decided how "pretense" is different from "pretext."

This usage is: Um, good luck.

I live in Pasadena, California—walking distance from the Rose Parade route. Every New Year's morning, I wake up to see my street lined with strange cars—only half of them containing passed-out relatives. The rest are people who drove from all over Southern California that morning to drink in the thrilling Rose Parade sights—everything from the "Casagrande for Rose Queen" sign on my lawn to the backs of forty thousand heads blocking their view of the floats.

I don't live close enough to smell Bob Eubanks's cologne (I hear it's a French fragrance, Eau du Maique Woupee), but I am close enough to hear the distinct sound of yawning.

Recently, one of the public radio stations ran a story alleging that the parade is directly responsible for countless people moving to Southern California every year. TV viewers see the sun and the blue skies and the eighteen-year-old girls wearing tiaras and think: That's the place for me.

What these people don't know is that they're lured here under false "pretenses." If they could see footage of Colorado Boulevard just ten hours before or ten hours later, the Southern California population would be much lower.

The night before the Rose Parade, New Year's Eve, Colorado Boulevard is lined for miles with thousands of people camping right in the street. They're cooking hot dogs on hibachis in front of the bank. They're running into traffic spraying Silly String on cars in front of the drugstore. And, my favorite, they're sleeping on the hard concrete in front of the window of the very comfy-looking mattress store.

After the parade, the bodies clear out, revealing what they left behind: garbage. Miles and miles of uninterrupted garbage that (and my hat's off to Pasadena for this one) is *completely* gone by January 2.

So a parade watcher's picture of Southern California in general and Pasadena in particular is all about timing. Just like segues into grammar topics.

As I said, the people who are inspired by the parade to move here do so under false pretenses. And I'd argue that *The Associated Press Stylebook* followers are similarly victimized regarding the difference between "pretense" and "pretext."

Chicago, Fowler's, Garner's, The Elements of Style, The Elephants of Style, Lapsing into a Comma, Usage and Abusage, The Careful Writer, The Dictionary of Disagreeable English, and *Word Court* don't see the need to distinguish between "pretense" and "pretext." But *The Associated Press Stylebook* does.

A "pretext," *AP* tells us, "is something that is put forward to conceal a truth." A "pretense," it says, "is a false show, a more overt act intended to conceal personal feelings."

What's that, you say? Not exactly crystal clear? Well, they do give a couple examples: "He was discharged for tardiness, but the reason given was only a pretext for general incompetence." "My profuse compliments were all pretense."

I'd argue that *AP* is acting under false pretenses—talking as if the words are totally distinct, even though they're not—except that the term "false pretenses" creates a mess all its own. We'll get to that in a minute.

First, let's see what the dictionary says about "pretense" and "pretext." *Webster's New World College Dictionary* says a "pretense" is "1. a claim, esp. an unsupported one, as to some distinction or accomplishment; pretension; 2. a false claim or profession; 3. a false show of something; 4. a pretending, as at play; make-believe. 5. a false reason or plea; pretext."

Did you catch that last word?

A "pretext," *Webster's* says, is "1. a false reason or motive put forth to hide the real one; excuse; 2. a cover-up; front."

So clearly, there's some overlap. But if you want to draw a line between the two, perhaps you should distill *AP*'s advice down to: "Pretext" conceals a truth, while "pretense" conceals feelings.

And that brings us back to the term "false pretenses." Considering that the word "false" is part of *Webster's* definition of "pretense," it seems to me that using the two together would be totally redundant.

But this isn't stopping people, according to a Google search. While the term "on the pretense" generates 94,200 hits and "on the pretext" generates 712,000, "false pretenses" pulls in a whopping 1,210,000 hits.

So does popularity reign supreme? I'll let you know as soon as I'm voted Rose Queen.

PART V

Pronoun Pains

55

Here's the thing <u>which</u> still stings.

This usage is: Highly !@%!&*! debatable.

In *Grammar Snobs Are Great Big Meanies*, I suggested that the English language was invented by Satan himself and that Simon Cowell and Linda Tripp were his cronies. I hinted at a correlation between conservative political punditry and uptight, anal, mean-spirited superiority. I speculated as to what might have crawled up William Safire's butt and died (a fanny-loving phoenix bug). I defamed copy editors, Jude Law, and the entire city of Newport Beach, California. I slipped in what I like to believe is the single dirtiest joke ever to appear in a grammar book (suggesting a new setup for the punch line "eats, shoots and leaves" that begins "A panda walks into a brothel . . ."). Oh, and I said that "which" is reserved for nonrestrictive clauses.

And of all those "bring-it-on," "make-my-day," "Hey, Jude, I called you a girly-man" remarks, only one drew the ire of critics and curmudgeons. Lots of ire.

Can you guess? Yes, I got a letter from the Fanny-Loving Phoenix Bug Antidefamation League explaining in no uncertain terms that they wouldn't touch Safire's behind with a ten-foot probe. But they were nice about it. The real crankcases were the people who took issue with the "which" business—to the max.

The first such comment came from a British blogger infuriated at my suggestion that Brits seem more inclined than Americans to use "which" to introduce restrictive clauses such as "I read" in "A blog which I read was written by a prissy fussbudget." (I'll explain restrictive and nonrestrictive clauses shortly.) On the contrary, the blogger wrote angrily, British people are every bit as observant of this important distinction as are Americans. (I'm paraphrasing a bit. He wasn't quite so nice about it.) I checked my *Chicago Manual of Style*, saw "In British English, writers and editors seldom observe the distinction between the two words," and decided to chalk the whole thing up to one blogger's "which" hunt.

But what came next was even better. A handful of highbrow types pounced on the opportunity to prove their superiority on the "which" issue. For example, one accused me of "joining the snob faction" on "(the fakest rule of all) limiting 'which' to non-restrictive clauses."

The Associated Press Stylebook, *The Chicago Manual of Style*, Strunk and White's *The Elements of Style*, *Lapsing into a Comma*, and many others say that "which" is reserved for nonrestrictive clauses. *Garner's* favors this distinction, and even *The Oxford English Grammar* could be said to lean this way.

A number of PhD linguists and their toadies disagree. They say that the best writers use "which" for restrictive clauses all the time. Therefore, they say, the whole distinction is artificial and misinformed (they prefer the word "stupid," but I like mine better).

So what's a guy or gal like you to do? Know the difference, pick a side, and either way prepare to be pummeled.

The best way to understand the difference between a restrictive clause and a nonrestrictive clause is that the former cannot be removed from a sentence without messing up the main point of that sentence.

Take "The shoes that I wore yesterday are more comfortable than these shoes."

Remove the information introduced by "that"—in other words, take out "that I wore yesterday"—and you're left with: "The shoes are more comfortable than these shoes." And that doesn't contain enough information to convey a complete thought because we don't know which shoes are being referred to. Therefore, the clause "that I wore yesterday" is essential to the meaning of the sentence because it restricts the phrase "the shoes"—narrows it down to something more specific.

Now consider "The shoes, which are a size too small, are very comfortable." The main point of the sentence is "The shoes are very comfortable." The stuff introduced by "which" can be lifted right out of the sentence without muddying this main point. It's extra information. An aside. It may be essential information to the reader, but it's not essential to the primary point of the sentence.

And if you noticed the commas in that last example, well, that's another clue. Commas set off parenthetical information, and nonrestrictive clauses are essentially parenthetical information, so traditionalists point out that "which" clauses are the ones set off by commas.

So if you use "which" to introduce a restrictive clause, as in "The shoes which I wore yesterday . . ." your choice will draw frowns from just about every copy editor in the country. But if you write a book in which you tell people they shouldn't use "which" this way, you'll experience a whole new level of which-iness.

56

When it comes to talking apes, I like <u>these ones</u>.

This usage is: Ugly but grammatical.

Some people, it seems, possess an innate sense of justice and an intrinsic urge to right society's wrongs. I am one of them, as the following example will irrefutably prove.

For a brief, shining moment during my childhood, the wildly popular *Planet of the Apes* movies were spun off into a *Planet of the Apes* television series. As a fan of all things furry that can also talk (which explains my later obsession with Steve Carell), I was shocked and devastated when the *Planet of the Apes* TV series was cancelled after a single season in 1974. I was so devastated, in fact, that I took it to the streets.

I marched from house to house on my street in Pinellas Park, Florida, clipboard in hand, asking neighbors to sign my petition to return *Planet of the Apes* to the airwaves.

So as you can see, I'm a born crusader with a keen sense of justice. Which is probably why I evolved into the type of person who goes apespit when I see grammar snobs using language to mess with people's heads.

Take, for example, the idea that you can't say "these ones" or "those ones." People who use these constructions do so without thinking much of it. But then someone comes along and puts these words under a microscope. Next thing you know you're dazed, struck dumb, and at the mercy of a bunch of monkeys.

"Here's the one that makes me cringe: 'These ones' or 'Those ones,'" writes a blogger going by the handle KEF. "Example: Sally: 'Suzy, which jeans did you end up buying at that fantastic sale?' Suzy: 'Oh, I bought these ones.' Throw up in my mouth . . . everytime [*sic*]."

At times, these kinds of criticism are so impassioned, so over the top, that we start to think maybe they're right. Maybe a plural like "these" or "those" is completely illogical in front of something so obviously meant to be singular as "one." Think about it long enough and you realize that you don't have the first clue what rules might govern such uses or where to turn for help.

But this tactic is as incorrect and, I daresay, as unjust as relegating intelligent human beings to an oppressed underclass subservient to a bunch of primates (far be it from me to point out the parallel).

Word Court author Barbara Wallraff argues that "ones" is perfectly grammatical (think: "There are ones I like and ones I don't like"). Further, she adds, "these" can function not only as a pronoun but also as an adjective. Therefore, she says of "these," "There's no grammatical reason why it shouldn't be allowed to modify the pronoun 'ones.'"

I don't remember what happened to my *Planet of the Apes* petition drive. I'm sure that the page containing three or four mercy signatures ended up in the trash bin right along with Roddy McDowall's chimp suit and Charlton Heston's career. But even though I failed in my crusade for quality television (thank heaven), at least I can continue the fight for all those who would say of the best *Apes* episodes: "Those ones were awesome."

57

He is smarter than *me.*

This usage is: Traditionally considered wrong, but now widely accepted.

There are a lot of people in the world—scary people—who would like to force you and me to say, "Oh, you're so much smarter than I," and, "Lance Armstrong is a better athlete than he."

Feel free to resent those people. I do. I resent them in part because, from a traditional perspective, they're right. "He is more brilliant than me" should be "than I" because technically you're saying "than I am."

All of this has to do with the fact that "than" is first and foremost a conjunction. But in sentences like our example, it's acting as a preposition. Prepositions take nouns or pronouns as objects, but a conjunction in a context like this introduces a whole clause, verb and all. That's how you know that "than I" is implying a verb, "am."

In other words, "than" is your clue that a verb has been dropped and that, therefore, you need a subject, "I," to go with that implied verb "am": "He is more brilliant than I *am.*" (Note the verb "am," which must be preceded by the subject form "I" and not the object form "me.") "Lance Armstrong is a better athlete than he is." (Note the verb "is," which must be preceded by "he" and not "him.")

And that's why, traditionally, the sticklers for this position have been right. But their reign of terror is drawing to a close.

Respected style experts including Partridge and Garner, as well as my *Webster's*, say it's okay to write "than me" in informal situations that would otherwise call for an "I." Lots of others agree.

But regardless of which approach you take, be careful.

Consider: "Dad loves you more than I" versus "Dad loves you more than me." In both cases, a verb is implied. But a very different meaning hangs in the balance. "Dad loves you more than I" suggests "more than *I love you*." "Dad loves you more than me" suggests "more than *he loves me*."

In the first case, the pronoun introduced by "than" is the subject of an action, so it takes the subject form "I." But in the second case, the pronoun is the object of the action, so it gets "me."

And that should be enough to convince you to do as I do: Ignore the old school rule in all but the most formal contexts. Then no one can say you're doing any worse than me.

58

He is more experienced than <u>myself</u>.

This usage is: Wrong.

*I*n my ongoing war against grammar snobbery, I encounter a lot of people whose position can be summed up as follows: Gee, I really don't want to be labeled a grammar snob—to have to accept that I'm a bad person just because I enjoy ridiculing others' grammar even when I'm wrong. But I don't want to give up ridiculing others' grammar. What can I do?

And for them, I have two words: Give birth.

Just as motherhood is the ultimate license to criticize hairstyles, taste in music, and college majors such as English and philosophy, it's also the ultimate license to dispense unsolicited language advice, including wrong language advice, with a major dose of attitude.

I know that becoming a parent sounds like a drastic solution, but any true grammar snob will agree: The right to run around insulting people for using "wrong" as an adverb even though it is an adverb is well worth one little episiotomy. Once the stitches are out, you'll have for the rest of your life the ironclad defense, "I'm telling you this because I love you, you clod."

(Let's pause here to call our therapists. . . . And we're back.)

If you decide to take this tack, you'll want to start small. Begin with a common parental beef that can be put into simple terms—

for example, reflexives such as "myself"—before moving on to giving completely bad advice.

A reader of my column named Barbara demonstrates:

"'How are you?' will absolutely elicit the answer, 'Fine and yourself?' or, 'Please get in touch with Mary or myself,' etc. This common error makes me grind my teeth!"

As much as I'd like to respond with a whole lot of sass-back, I have to admit that Barbara's advice is pretty sound.

If you're rusty, here's a helpful guideline. If it can be replaced with "me," don't use "myself." If it can be replaced with "you," don't use "yourself." If it can be replaced with "him," don't use "himself." And so on.

Occasionally, you may encounter a case where "myself" could be replaced by "me" but then your sentence wouldn't sound as good. The most famous example is "such as myself" instead of "such as me." In those cases, you're probably better off following your instincts. Some will scoff, but some experts will back you up.

That's the simple approach. If you want a more thorough understanding of "reflexive pronouns" and you're sufficiently hopped up on some mother's little helper such as espresso, here goes.

"Reflexive pronouns"—the ones that end with "self" or "selves"—have just a few basic uses.

First and most important, a reflexive works with another noun or pronoun in a sentence to "co-refer" to the same entity.

Consider "I see myself in a better job." In this sentence, "I" and "myself" refer to the same person. They co-refer.

This "co-referring" reflexive can be any one of a number of different parts of speech. It can be a direct object, as in the foregoing example. It can be an indirect object, as in "He sent himself an e-mail." (In case you're rusty, the direct object of the verb here is "e-mail" because it's the actual object of the action "send." The indirect object can trick you into thinking it's the direct object of the verb because it happens to come immediately after it. But the thing being sent, in this case, is the e-mail.)

The reflexive can also be the complement of a linking verb like "to be," as in "You should always be yourself."

And it can follow the word "by" to refer to someone or something performing an action in a verb: "I can get dressed all by myself."

Don't be tricked by imperative sentences, or commands: "Don't overestimate yourself." In imperative sentences the subject is implied. In this case it's "you." So "yourself" is working with "you" to co-refer to the same person, even though we don't see or say the word "you."

And, of course, reflexives can also be used just for emphasis. Of course, that use can sometimes be annoying. That's why I, myself, try to avoid it.

59

<u>Whom</u> shall I say is calling (the media biased)?

This usage is: Wrongo.

$\mathcal{S}$ince it's been pages and pages since I last ranted about so-called "media bias," I will explain the proper use of "whom" by sharing with you some insights into a typical week of a newspaper reporter.

Day 1: Write a story about a murder committed by a prominent Republican.

Day 2: Get a nasty e-mail about your liberal bias.

Day 3: Write a story about a murder committed by a prominent Democrat.

Day 4: Get a nasty e-mail about your liberal bias because the article didn't include the phrase "a crime typical of those morally bankrupt liberals."

Day 5: Write a story about a Republican who runs off to Tahiti with the life savings of thousands of desperately poor senior citizens. Aim for balance by mentioning what a wonderful guy the Republican swindler had been because he once petted a puppy.

Day 6: Get a nasty e-mail about your liberal bias because you neglected to mention that the puppy was black.

Day 7: Donate $1,000 to your local Republican
congressional candidate.

Day 7, moments later: Get accused of liberal bias
because your check had a picture of the endan-
gered manatee on it.

That's why this chapter is not about President Bush's "whom"
mistake in the statement "Khalid Sheikh Muhammad sought out
young men from Southeast Asia, whom he believed would not
arouse as much suspicion."

No, indeed. This is about NPR reporter Corey Flintoff's similar but somehow far more egregious pronoun failure in reporting
about a presidential race in Haiti: "The U.S. expects to work with
whomever wins this election."

Like the president, Flintoff needed a pronoun that was the
object of one clause (The U.S. will work with *him*) but the subject of another (*he* wins this election). And they both opted for
the object pronoun instead of the subject. But Flintoff's choice is
somehow far more offensive in a manatee-loving, refusing-to-
report-that-God-is-a-Republican kind of way.

Here's what those Flintoffs in the liberal media don't want
you to know: Whenever you need a pronoun to serve as the
object of one clause but the subject of another clause, the subject
form wins.

A clause, in case the liberal education system didn't teach it
to you, is best thought of as a portion of a sentence or a whole
sentence that contains a subject and a verb. In the common but
incorrect sentence "Whom shall I say is calling," one of the clauses
is "I say" but another is "who/whom is calling." The verbs in both
these clauses need subjects ("he is calling") and not objects ("him
is calling"). That's why it's "who is calling" even when it's the
object of another verb or preposition.

The correct sentence, therefore, is, "*Who* shall I say is calling," just as Flintoff should have said, ". . . with *whoever* wins this election," and just as the president's speechwriters, if not infiltrated by liberally biased subversives, would have written, ". . . *who* he believed would not arouse as much suspicion."

I listen to <u>whoever's</u> music is on the radio.

This usage is: Okay, but "whosever" may be a better choice.

Like you, I'm sick of "who," "whom," and all things related to them. But there's one more thing we should all note. So we'll make this quick.

There exists the word "whosever." Traditionally, this was the only right choice in cases like the sentence at the top of this page, though now "whoever's" has gained a lot of respectability.

Says *The Chicago Manual of Style*, in a sentiment seconded by *Garner's* and *Fowler's*, "*Whosever; whoever's*. The first is correct in formal writing, 'We need to talk to whosever bag that is'; the second is acceptable in casual usage, 'Whoever's dog got into our garbage can should clean up the mess.'"

Note that when you want not the possessive but the contraction, "whoever's" is rock solid: "Whoever's tall enough can ride this roller coaster." "Whoever's" can always stand in for "whoever is" or "whoever has." But if it's the possessive you want, note that "whosever" might be a better option.

Oh, and if you ever find yourself tempted to make "whomever" into the possessive "whomever's," just don't. Use "whosever" or "whoever's" instead.

You can address readers in the second person.

This usage is: Correct.

Yes, I know what your English teacher told you when you were writing your paper on the underappreciated artistry of '80s band Kajagoogoo. I know she said to manufacture a subject for your sentences ("the Kajagoogoo fan") and refer to your subject as a "he" or a "she" throughout your timelessly riveting essay: "The Kajagoogoo fan should subscribe to the band's newsletter to learn fascinating trivia. In it, she'll see that Kajagoogoo is indeed a musical force to be reckoned with, guaranteed to crank out hits for decades to come."

Sure, that's one way to do it, but does it really do Kajagoogoo justice when you could have written, with far more impact: "*You* can find fascinating trivia in Kajagoogoo's newsletter. Here *you*'ll see that Kajagoogoo is indeed a musical force to be reckoned with. . . ."

In the most formal writing, sometimes it's best to avoid the second person. But anyone who tells you there's a rule against using "you" is lying out his kaja and/or his googoo.

In fact, in *Garner's Modern American Usage* you'll find this so-called rule listed under "s" for "superstitions." Garner quotes two books, including one called *Style and Readability in Business Writing*: "Not only does the use of *you* eliminate the passive and make sentences more readable, it directs the writing where it should be directed: to the reader. The 'you attitude' is reader-oriented rather than writer-oriented."

So you don't have to worry about this anymore. Indeed, when you pitch a retrospective article to *Rolling Stone* magazine, feel free to write, "You know you still love Kajagoogoo as much as I do."

62

Of all the sticklers out there, none <u>are</u> more rabid than the "none are" prohibitionists.

This usage is: Okay.

*I*t's pitch-black. You're on a stage. All you can hear is the labored breathing of your scene partner and a muffled scream that you hope is only in your head and not coming out of your mouth.

You have no lines. You have no script. You have just a vague suggestion from an audience member: "They work at Target." You frantically search your memory banks for humor fodder from your past Target trips, but you can't come up with anything more original than "Chia Pet."

Lights up.

Welcome to the terrifying world of improv, where the quick-witted can rise to incredible fame and the not-so-quick-witted discover they're better off writing grammar books.

In my years of studying improv at the Groundlings and elsewhere, I saw a lot of great improvisers—both on stage and in class. And I'm proud to report that, of all the brilliant improvising I've seen in my life, the best I've ever seen was done by me. I'm less proud to report that it was done in my head, hours or days after the actual performance.

So I can honestly say that, of all the brilliant improvisers I've seen, *none are* as clever in a split second as I am given a week and a half. And I can also say that, as a result of my Monday-morning improviser abilities, I've had plenty of free time to learn about verb conjugations with "none."

Some people cringe when you say stuff like "None of my friends *attend* my performances." Their problem is the verb. They say it should be "attends" as in "he attends," instead of "attend" as in "they attend." These people are stuck on the belief that "none" means "not one," which is singular and therefore requires a singular verb.

This sounds sensible until you start opening books. *Chicago, Fowler's, Garner's, The Careful Writer, Usage and Abusage, The Elements of Style, The Elephants of Style, Word Court,* and *The Oxford English Grammar* agree that "none" sometimes means "not any" and therefore *can* take a plural verb.

The Associated Press Stylebook is the only one that gets a little strict on the subject: "Use the plural verb only if the sense is 'no two' or 'no amount': 'None of the consultants agree on the same approach.' 'None of the taxes have been paid.'"

This would be pretty convincing if *AP* didn't stand completely alone on this point.

So what should you do? Ask yourself whether your "none" means "not one" or "not any" and conjugate accordingly. If both those options work fine and you still don't know what to choose, consider this: The first two definitions of "none" in my *Webster's* say it means "not one." The third says it means "not any." So, when in doubt, you may want to opt for the preferred definition. Because, of all the Chia Pet–loving wankers out there, none is likely to wank at you for saying "none is." (Though there are plenty who could rightly ream you for going out on a Chia Pet joke.)

63

Was it Horton <u>that</u> heard the Who?

This usage is: Grammatical but not ideal.

*H*orton Hears a Who is a darling children's book about an elephant who discovers tiny people-like creatures living right under his trunk. *Hortense Hears a That* is a book I just made up about an even-longer-nosed creature that goes around sniffing out "whos" and, when it finds "thats" instead, tramples whoever used them.

Take this blogger named Janet: "Here's my grammar peeve: People who use 'that' when they really mean 'who.' . . . Using 'that' is sloppy, lazy, and unacceptable."

Here's the homily of these Hortenses: "Who" or "whom," they say, is necessary whenever talking about a person. "That," they insist, applies only to things and not people.

"There's the girl *who* sells seashells by the seashore," they say. Not, "There's the girl *that* sells seashells."

I was taught this myself, so I can't help but prefer "who" to "that" in such cases. But that doesn't mean "that" is wrong, my sources say.

The Oxford English Grammar explains that "who" is always personal (meaning it refers to a person or possibly an animal), "which" is always nonpersonal, but "that" is "used for both personal and non-personal reference."

Garner's also gives permission to use "that" for people, though perhaps a little more reluctantly: "*Who* is the relative pronoun for human beings (though *that* is also acceptable)."

Partridge and Bernstein agree. Fowler agrees in some cases. But Wallraff puts it best: "The word *that* has a long history of referring to people as well as things. This usage may in some contexts sound a bit crude, but it is not ungrammatical, and it can sometimes offer a writer a graceful way out, as in, "Did she say it was a man or a book that she curled up with last night?"

As I said, when talking about a person, I usually prefer "who." It's more precise and often clearer. But if Hortense hears a "that," that's okay, too.

64

It's companies like Horton Biosciences <u>who</u> make Whoburgers so popular.

This usage is: Wrong (so wrong).

A company is not a who. A country is not a who. An animal is sometimes a who, usually when it's a who to you. But inanimate things shouldn't be referred to with the relative pronoun "who."

That's what makes it different from "that," which we saw in the last chapter is a lot more flexible. "That" can be used for people or for things. But "who" doesn't swing that way, say *Oxford, AP*, Walsh, Fiske, and *Garner's*.

Who knew?

PART VI

Indecent Prepositions

65

It's not too big <u>of</u> a deal.

This usage is: Better without the "of."

We Americans are proud of our free elections, but we all have a shameful little secret: Anytime we have to vote in a small-time judicial race or for one of those dizzying ballot initiatives supported by Americans for Better Schools but opposed by Citizens for School Betterment, we all secretly wish we lived in one of those countries where nice men wearing berets and army fatigues do all the decision making for us. (Say what you will about Fidel Castro, Moammar Kadafi, and Idi Amin, there's no way they could know any less about John Q. Judgely's qualifications for the bench than I do.)

So I'll confess that, as much as I dis the style and grammar mavens, sometimes I'm just grateful to find someone to tell me what to do.

This is one of those times.

We can spend our whole lives pondering whether the "of" is necessary in "It's not too big of a deal" without ever learning the truth or even where to turn. It's not like your eleventh-grade English teacher was getting into this stuff as she taught you to read *Curious George Goes to the Beach*. (Disclaimer: Example composed by a product of Florida public schools. Your educational experience may vary.) So when you find an authority who's willing to think it out and write it out, well, that's one time when it seems pretty wise to submit your will.

"Intrusive 'of.' The word 'of' often intrudes where it doesn't idiomatically belong, as in 'not that big of a deal' (read 'not that big a deal')," *Garner's Modern American Usage* tells us.

It's an answer, so I'll take it.

"It wasn't too long a walk" is therefore preferable to "too long *of* a walk." "Jack didn't give James too hard a time" is preferable to "too hard *of* a time."

I must muddy the waters, though, by mentioning that "much" is different. "Much" usually works in idioms with "of," so "too much of a good thing" is clearly right and other "too much of" constructions are often right or at least defended.

But unless you're working with "much" or another word that buddies around with "of," usually you can leave "of" out altogether. And if we can accept this, perhaps we can admit there are times when participating in a democracy seems too tall an order.

66

All <u>of</u> my exes live in the greater Houston metropolitan area.

This usage is: Okay, but maybe not ideal.

There's a song titled "All My Ex's Live in Texas." It's by an artist named George Strait on an album titled *50 Number Ones.*

I'm not sure why Strait considered the residences of his former wives and lovers worth singing about (unless, of course, it's some cryptic communiqué to a hired hit man). But the song raises some even more curious issues. Wouldn't "exes" be better than "ex's"? Wouldn't "all of" be better than just "all"? Wouldn't the album be more appropriately titled *50 Number Twos*?

It is with great confidence that I can answer "yes" to two of those questions. But that "all" versus "all of" isn't as cut-and-dried.

While "all" and "all of" both have a place, some experts say the Strait way is better.

"The more formal construction is to omit 'of' and write, when possible, 'All the attempts failed,'" writes Bryan Garner.

But there are two instances in which your "of" is as indispensable to an English speaker as bourbon and self-pity are to a country singer.

First, you want to keep the "of" whenever your "all" comes before a pronoun. That is, you want "all of them" instead of "all them."

Second, you want to keep the "of" whenever your "all" comes before a possessive: "I wonder whether all of George's exes are concentrated in the greater Houston metropolitan area."

These are not hard-and-fast rules—just recommendations by *Garner's* that are echoed in *Chicago, The Careful Writer,* and elsewhere. "All," they agree, is both an adjective and a noun, so you can use it either way you like.

But if you're playing it safe, I would add to Garner's yet a third circumstance in which you want to keep your "of," before "which": "I listened to the 50 songs, all *of* which instilled in me a much deeper appreciation of disco."

Look <u>towards</u> the future.

This usage is: Incredibly unpopular.

*I*f language were a popularity contest, "toward" would be the captain of the football team, while "towards" would be the guy who dreams of one day making the chess team but for now just eats bugs under the bleachers (or, as I called him, "prom date").

In America, at least, everybody likes "toward." But nobody wants anything to do with "towards." "I personally find . . . the *s* on the end of words like *upwards, downwards,* and especially *towards* superfluous and downright silly," writes a user at Fireflyfans.net.

The Associated Press Stylebook says use "toward." *Fowler's, The Careful Writer, Garner's,* and *Chicago* all agree that, in American English, "toward" is the way to go.

"The preferred form is without the *s* in American English, with it in British English," the *Chicago* authors write. "The same is true for other directional words, such as *upward, downward, forward,* and *backward,* as well as *afterward.*"

The dictionaries don't like "towards," either. They act like they barely even know it exists, snubbing it like a lead cheerleader snubs a flat-chested freshman. (That's right, Tracy. I didn't forget.)

We divided the money <u>between</u> the four of us.

This usage is: Incorrect, according to some; not so cut-and-dried, according to others.

$\mathcal{F}$or this chapter on the difference between "between" and "among," I will be employing the help of my lovely assistant, Tibor the kitten (pronounced "TEE-bore"). Tibor's grammar smarts stem, in part, from the fact that he was named after a *Simpsons* episode—*The Simpsons* being, according to one insightful and good-looking reviewer, "the most grammatically and linguistically savvy show on television."

In season four, Marge decides to get a job alongside husband Homer at the nuclear power plant. Homer gives her his best advice: "If something goes wrong at the plant, blame the guy who can't speak English. Ah, Tibor! How many times have you saved my butt?" Later in the show, when this bit is long forgotten, Homer is upset over something completely unrelated: Marge has been promoted—to a position above Homer's.

Homer whines, "I'm used to seeing people promoted ahead of me: friends, co-workers, Tibor."

This joke paid off a third time when, months or years later, I noticed in the show's credits an animator and layout artist named Tibor—a real guy who may or may not speak enough English to realize his co-workers were teasing him.

Thus, an otherwise perfectly dignified Hungarian name has become a punch line to ridicule a poor, unsuspecting kitten.

My Tibor, the kitten, will help resolve our usage conundrum. Here's how. I am gathering up all of my books that discuss the difference between "among" and "between." These include *The Associated Press Stylebook*, *The Dictionary of Disagreeable English*, Barbara Wallraff's *Word Court*, and *The Elements of Style*—all of which say that "between" describes relationships between pairs, whereas "among" describes relationships between three or more. It's "*between* you and me," they say, but "The money was divided *among* the four ticket holders." These books add, however, that whenever you're talking about one-on-one interactions within a larger group, "between" is the one you want. "For example," Wallraff writes, "no matter how many acts a play has, intermissions occur between them, not among them."

My stack of books also includes experts who take the opposite position, so I'm also gathering up *Fowler's Modern English Usage*, *Garner's Modern American Usage*, *The Chicago Manual of Style*, and *Lapsing into a Comma*—all of which say this two-versus-more-than-two-distinction just isn't so.

Now I am arranging all these books in a circle on the floor. . . . Now I am cramming Tibor into a sequined leotard. . . . And finally, I am placing him in the center of all the books to see which one he'll select by walking to it first.

Drum roll, please.

And Tibor is sitting down. He's looking at me as if to ask, "What am I doing in this ridiculous leotard?" He's turning a little to the right. And, oh, look at that, folks—he's taking a step toward *Chicago*! Wait, wait. He's turning back! Something in the other direction has caught his eye—something outside the circle. It's his food dish!

Tibor's leaning back on his haunches as if to . . . yes! yes! He's springing. He's in the air! And he has landed in front of . . . Pro Plan Salmon and Ocean Fish!

There you have it, folks—a resolution to this conundrum that's as scientific and conclusive as any offered by our nation's finest linguistic minds.

So, if you like the idea of using "among" for more than two and "between" for just two, by all means use them accordingly. If you don't like this distinction, you can get away with ignoring it, assuming you're willing to catch some grief. But if you'll opt for nothing less than a scientifically determined solution, use "among" only when referring to stinky ground fish parts.

Ah, Tibor! How many times have you saved my butt?

69

A preposition is something you can end a sentence <u>with</u>.

This usage is: Fine.

*I*f I were God (which I'm not), I'd bring Winston Churchill back to life—just long enough to book him on *The Colbert Report*.

And if I had my way (which I would, on account of being God), I think it'd go a little something like this:

> *Host Stephen Colbert:* Now, Mr. Churchill. Of all the pithy sayings and incisive quotes attributed to you, I have to say my all-time favorite is your comment about the so-called "rule" that you can't end a sentence with a preposition. Let's see, your exact words were . . . (Colbert riffles through notes)
>
> *Churchill:* . . . Ah yes, "That is the type of pedantry up with which I will not put!"
>
> *Colbert:* Hmm. That's funny. My notes here say the quote is "the type of *arrant* pedantry up with which I will not put." You must have left out the "arrant" just now, huh?
>
> *Churchill:* Uh, indeed.
>
> *Colbert:* (Riffling through more notes) No, wait. Wait. Here on this card it says, "This is *nonsense* up with which I will not put."

Churchill: Uh . . . Um . . .

Colbert: (Still riffling) And look. Here's another: "This is *the sort of bloody nonsense* up with which I will not put."

Churchill: Um . . . yes. That's right.

Colbert: (Reaching the bottom of his stack of notes) Actually, it says here that you may not have ever said anything of the sort.

Churchill: Uh, well, yes. I did say it. And I tell you that in all truthiness.

Colbert: Ah! Touché, sir. But you're not getting off the hook that easily.

Churchill: Look! A bear!

That's right, folks, you heard it here first unless you've already heard it somewhere else: The most popular, most revered, most repeated linguistics-related quotation of all time (with the only possible exception being "grammar snobs are great big meanies") may be not only misquoted but attributed to the wrong guy.

Benjamin J. Zimmer, a language expert cited in the book *Far From the Madding Gerund*, has researched the origins of this famous quotation and concluded that not only has the quote shown up in many different forms, it's quite possible that Churchill never said it at all.

The first incarnation of the quote that Zimmer found was dated 1942 and was in a piece by an unnamed writer for the *Strand* magazine. Churchill was also a writer for the *Strand*, but Churchill was famous. So chances are that if these words had been Churchill's, his name would have been on them. More likely, some linguists conclude, somebody else penned this famous zinger and somehow got robbed of the credit. (Like I'm sure to get robbed of credit for pithily coining the term to describe this phenomenon: "misquotiness," defined as attributing words to whoever you'd like to believe said them rather than finding out who actually said them.)

Also, the famous quotation has shown up in many different forms—all attributed to Churchill. So until someone can prove that he said at least one of them, I'm going to stop crediting Churchill with this clever quip. I will not, however, stop spreading the word about its message.

Here's what you need to know about ending sentences with prepositions—little words like "at," "to," "with," "in," and "on": There's no rule against it. You can do so anytime you like.

But it's not always your best choice. Prepositions are normally thought of as taking objects. In the sentence "You go shopping with her," the preposition is "with" and its object is "her." So when you write "She's the one you go shopping with," you're sort of separating the preposition "with" from its object. And that can get awkward. That's why some people prefer "with whom you go shopping."

One more quick example and then we can all get back to watching *Comedy Central*: "That's the house you live in" separates the preposition "in" from its object, "the house." Because, you live *in the house*. That's why some people opt for a solution like "in which you live."

So whenever possible, you want your object to follow its partner as quickly as possible. But the decision is up to you. To defile yet another Churchillism, sometimes ending a sentence with a preposition "is the worst possible form except for all the others."

70

This letter is in <u>regards</u> to your advertisement.

This usage is: Despised by the big guys.

Many of the chapters in this book talk about disputes in the language world and try to help you navigate the experts' conflicting advice. Not this chapter. On "in regards to" there is no dispute among my team of experts. They all hate it:

> *In regard to.* This is the phrase, not *in regards to.*
> —*Chicago*

> The singular noun is correct.   —*Garner's*

> *In regard to.* Often wrongly written *in regards to.*
> —*The Elements of Style*

> *In regards to* . . . is an example of egregious English.
> —*The Dictionary of Disagreeable English*

Usage and Abusage agrees, and *Fowler's* registers its disapproval of "in regards to" by refusing to even mention it in its entry on what it deems the correct "in regard to."

Of course, that's just from the experts. If you want to know what the masses think of these two terms, a Google search sheds some light. "In regard to" scored about 9.9 million hits. But "in regards to," at 9.5 million hits, was trailing so slightly that the Supreme Court could get away with declaring it the winner.

Still, those 9.9 million can be pretty vehement.

"I hate it when people say *in regards to*," writes a user at the SFGate Culture Blog. So now that you know how to avoid their wrath, you might as well do so.

And you might also want to note that "*with* regard to" works the same way, the experts say. Don't put that "s" on "regard." But the expression "as regards" does take the "s."

71

Where are you <u>at</u>?

This usage is: So hip it hurts (your chances of getting into a good college).

*I*f I were auditioning to appear in a youth-oriented cell phone ad, I would ask the receptionist, "Yo, where's the audition at?" I would ask the casting agent, "Where's the script at?" I would ask the producer, "Homes, where's my job at?"

No doubt these professionals would all respond, "Um, hello. This was a casting call for young hip people. Not for old nerdy people who think they can pass just by butchering the language. Where's your brain at?"

So that's why, when it comes to "where are you at," I'm not saying it's bad. I'm not saying anything that could destroy my dream of one day becoming the world's oldest MTV vee-jay. But I am saying that, if you want to be grammatical, don't say, "Where are you at?" (And no matter what you do, don't drop the "are": "Where you at?")

The "at" is just an extra word thrown in. It's not part of the standard grammatical construction. As such, it's redundant. "Where are you?" says it all quite nicely without "at." The "where" and the "are" contain built-in references to place or location that render the "at" unnecessary.

Some might argue that the version with the "at" has become an accepted idiom. Others might argue that it's a good way to add emphasis—a little oomph to pound home the importance of the location. I, personally, would argue that it's helpful in constructions such as "Where are we at on the Penske file?"

But, in most cases, unless you're trying to impress people who wear their pants below their patooties, drop the "at."

72

In behalf of the shareholders,
I accept this big check.

This usage is: Better changed to
"on behalf of," though
"in behalf of" has some uses, too.

*P*repositions—little words including "in" and "on"—have enormous power to make people feel stupid. We know that "in behalf of" sounds like a lame substitute for "on behalf of" in the example above, but we'd be hard pressed to explain why. Surely there must be some rule or at least some general guideline we should be able to follow anytime we don't know which preposition to use, right?

Wrong.

The Careful Writer author Theodore Bernstein puts it best: "The proper preposition is a matter of idiom; and idioms, if they do not come 'naturally,' must be either learned or looked up." Of course, there is no *Dictionary of Which Preposition to Use in Situations Where You See a Cell Phone Commercial and Want to Effectively Criticize the Phrase "Where You At?"* (at least not until I convince my publisher that there should be). So following Bernstein's advice to look stuff up isn't as easy as he makes it sound. My personal library contains just enough guidance to drive a person nuts. But amid the mess we can glean a better understanding of the difference between "in behalf of" and "on behalf of."

Bernstein, Garner, Wallraff, and *Chicago* say "on behalf of" means speaking for or representing someone else. "In behalf of" means helping someone else. So, "I speak *in* John's behalf" means

I'm trying to help him, but "I speak *on* John's behalf" means I'm speaking for him.

R. W. Burchfield, on behalf of H. W. Fowler, disagrees, even taking a rare potshot at Garner: "In American English *in behalf of* vies with *on behalf of* in the same two senses, though Garner (1987) insists that a distinction exists." Mee-ow. *Usage and Abusage* also says that the two terms justifiably overlap.

But most of us can agree that uses like "In behalf of Mr. Lucas, I accept this Oscar" sound perfectly horrible. The dictionary backs us up. While suggesting that both terms can mean "in the interest of," *Webster's* seems to think that only one can mean "speaking for" or "representing." For that meaning, *Webster's* says, you want "*on* behalf of."

And in behalf of English users everywhere, that's the best I can do to find a clear answer.

73

Don't listen to fuddy-duddies <u>like</u> this guy.

This usage is: Like, totally controversial (which means you can get away with it if you really want to).

𝒯he word "like" is like a box of chocolates: You never know when you're going to run into a nut.

For example, using "like" in any place where you could have used "such as" is likely to give certain people, like, a total hissy fit. Unfortunately for said hissy-fitters, lots of well-respected authorities, including the *New York Times*, say that "like" is as good as "such as" or better.

Compare the words of columnist James Kilpatrick to those of columnist Barbara Wallraff on these uses of "like":

> *Kilpatrick:* "Syntactical constipation. . . . Only the most slovenly writers will abandon an honest, unassuming *such as* in favor of a deceptive *like*."

> *Wallraff:* "A common superstition notwithstanding, *like* can also mean *such as*."

Since the grammar gods are still duking this one out, you should make it a point to know your audience.

When writing for a publication such as the *New Yorker*, stick with "such as." When writing a blog titled "Why Kanye West Can Kick Fitty's Butt," feel free to use "like."

But that's just the difference between "like" and "such as." There's a completely different war over whether you can use "like" in place of just plain-old "as."

Strunk and White, Robert Hartwell Fiske, and other authorities will tell you that "like" introduces only nouns or pronouns: "It tastes *like* chicken." But when a whole clause, verb and all, follows, you need "as": "Don't do *as* I do, do *as* I say."

Is there a consensus among the big shots on this one? Like, no way. *Fowler's Modern English Usage, Garner's Modern American Usage*, and some other books all leave some wiggle room—especially in informal writing and speech. So that means it's not, like, totally wrong. But that doesn't mean it's a good idea. These same authorities argue that, though it's becoming acceptable to use "like" as a conjunction, we're not there yet.

That touches on yet another important use of "like": "Like" is often a preposition, and pronouns that follow prepositions are always in object form. "Apes are so like us" is correct (for certain people especially) because "us" is an object. "Apes are so like we" is wrong because "we" is the subject form. And you can get away with saying "Apes are so like we are," awkward and informal as that is, with "like" acting as a conjunction introducing a whole clause, verb and all.

Take that a step further and you're clued in to a rule that will dazzle the most self-important former English majors in your office: Constructions like "He, like me, is a Weather Girls fan" also take an object ("me") instead of a subject ("I"). Again, the reason is due to that preposition "like." Here's another: "We, like them, are happy about the merger." Not: "We, like they." Awkward? You bet. But grammatically sound.

Of course, "like" isn't just a preposition. It has lots of other roles.

It can be a noun: "What are your likes and dislikes?"

It can be a verb: "I like Sir Mix-a-Lot and I cannot lie."

It can be an interjection—a "verbal tic"—used by young people to drive older people, like, totally insane: "Funyons are, like, totally delicious." But you don't want to use this "like" on the essay portion of your SATs.

And it can be used with forms of "to be" to create a synonym for "said" that is the keystone in a youth conspiracy to send parents and grandparents to an early grave: "I was like, 'No way!' And he was like, 'Yes, way!' "

Of course, those last two are pretty widely despised. But the verbal tic version of "like" has some surprising credentials for respectability. "In teenagers, the use is all but ubiquitous," *Garner's Modern American Usage* tells us. "In adults, it shows arrested development." (I, like, couldn't agree more.) What's more, this use of "like" dates back all the way to the late 1700s! So, for a youth trend, that's, like, seriously old.

74

**I've been a world-famous
blogger for <u>over</u> two weeks.**

This usage is: Fine, despite all those people
who would say you must use "more than."

𝓑logging is crazy stuff. When the trend first began, I couldn't
imagine anything crazier than some fifteen-year-old in Boise assuming that strangers would want to read about his struggle to
learn the oboe or his failed attempts at getting to second base.

Then I discovered something much, much crazier. People actually read them.

I've since come to understand some of the reasons behind all
the readers. For example, the current state of network TV. Sure,
a zitty kid journaling about his triumphs in fingering "Red River
Valley" sounds perfectly excruciating, unless your only alternative
is a rerun of *Yes, Dear*.

As a result, we have more blogs about more topics than you
can shake YouTube at. And grammar is no exception. Do a
Google search for "grammar peeves" and you'll see exactly what
I'm talking about. It seems there are more people out there rant-
ing about misuses of "they're" and "there" than there are people
actually misusing the words.

But the bigger problem is the fact that, as we've seen, the rant-
ers don't always know what they're talking about.

For example, one outrageous "abuse" of the language you
might read about on the web is people using "over" to mean "more
than" and "under" to mean "less than." Take this rant from a user

at the Commercials I Hate website: "One of my big peeves is the use of *over* to mean *more than*. 'We have been going there over two years.' I hate that."

The idea—one I, too, used to believe—is that "over" and "under" refer only to physical position. According to this argument, if you say you're "over fifty" it doesn't mean you're fifty-one or older. It means that you're physically suspended like Sandy Duncan over a cardboard cutout of the numerals five and zero.

And, as you probably guessed, this isn't quite right.

Yes, "more than" is more precise when emphasizing numbers or quantities: "Tyler struck out with more than two dozen girls last semester."

And lots of style authorities caution against using "over" instead of "more than," but there are plenty who defend it, as well: "*Over*: As an equivalent of *more than*, this word is perfectly good idiomatic English," *Chicago* tells us. *Fowler's* and *Garner's* agree. Partridge allows it in most cases. Only *AP* says to opt for "over" exclusively in spatial relationships and to stick to "more than" for numbers (a distinction Garner calls a "baseless crotchet").

What's more, sometimes experts argue that "over" is actually better—specifically when you're not emphasizing individual units. "The car was traveling at over eighty miles per hour," they say, is arguably better than "more than eighty miles per hour" because it puts the emphasis on overall speed and not on individual units.

In other words, because "more than" puts the emphasis on the countable units, "more than two years" might suggest three or four or five years. Whereas "over two years" allows for incremental increases—two years and one day, two years and one month, etc.

So, when in doubt, stick with "more than" or "less than." But if it sounds better to you, use "over" and "under" however you see fit.

75

I get bad editing advice <u>for</u> free.

This usage is: Not best, but not wrong either.

*O*ne day we'll all be dead. For most, this is a mixed bag. Sure, it's a bummer you're dead. But at least you'll get some relief from all the little nagging annoyances that haunt your personal and professional life every day—a Regis Philbin–free plane of existence some call heaven.

But not me. If my experience with writing a weekly grammar column is any indication, I'll be lying there in my grave with some language stickler's sensible shoes just inches above my face as she corrects real or perceived typos on my headstone with a red marker.

Certain people may love catching mistakes in newspapers and books, but there's nothing these types love more than catching mistakes in a grammar column. They love it so much, in fact, that they don't even bother to check whether they're really mistakes (suggesting that the red ink on my tombstone will leave me with something like "Here lays June, from who many people learned to never split infinitives").

In the years I've been writing my column, I've been called on the carpet for everything from using "wrong" as an adverb (which it is) to using "could care less" instead of "could not care less" (which is a little tougher to defend, on account of it stinks).

Most recently (in fact just a day before I began writing this wistful look forward to the inevitable) I got some serious grief for writing "for free."

"You have hit a sore spot with me . . . a familiar error," a reader named Jerry told me via e-mail. "[You wrote] 'some of the best resources are available for free on the Internet.' Something is free or free of charge, but not *for free.*"

Note that Jerry's e-mail was not qualified with "I think" or "I was taught" or "I'm pretty sure" or "according to my mama." It was a flat-out proclamation that I was wrong.

And if there's one thing I've learned in this brief reprieve from eternal oblivion, it's that most of the time when someone says a grammar or usage choice is "wrong," there's a good chance that he's wrongly overstating his case.

"*Free; for free.* Because *free* by itself can function as an adverb in the sense 'at no cost,' some critics reject the phrase *for free*," *Garner's Modern American Usage* tells us. "While it's true that *for free* is a casualism and a severely overworked ad cliché, the expression is far too common to be called an error. Sometimes the syntax all but demands it."

This seems to be the reigning attitude on "for free." None of the bosses fully sanction it, but most allow it sometimes.

And for good reason. As Wallraff points out, sometimes that little "for" really can help: "Pity the person who has written 'I wanted to get the car free.' One can't tell whether the writer has entered a sweepstakes or called a tow truck."

Here's a similar example from Garner: "Soft-dollar arrangements . . . include various services like research and information that big institutional clients receive for free from brokers."

Perhaps these clients would rather receive them "*free from* brokers," but that little "for" makes it clear that they're going to have to deal with a broker if they're going to avoid paying for the services.

Webster's allows "for free," too, as does *Fowler's*, which calls it "semi-humorous slang."

The biggest opponent is *Washington Post* copyediting guru Walsh, who says straight out: "You get something *free*, not *for free*. The technical reason is: It's an adverb, not a noun."

But while it may be "wrong" for a *Post* copy editor to allow "for free" on Walsh's watch, the rest of us are free to follow any guideline we like.

PART VII

Adjective Nauseam

How <u>fortuitous</u> that your Halliburton stock has skyrocketed.

This usage is: Bad.

*I*f you're looking for a word that means "fortunate" but is just—oh, I don't know—fancier, well, I have some unfortunate news: "Fortuitous" isn't it.

Think of "fortuitous" as meaning "accidental." Think of "fortunate" as the correct choice when you mean "lucky."

In *Chicago*'s words, "*Fortuitous* means 'by chance,' whether the fortune is good or bad. 'The rotten tree could have fallen at any time; it was just fortuitous that the victims drove by when they did.' *Fortunate* means 'blessed by good fortune.' 'We were fortunate to win the raffle.'"

My sources are unanimous on this, with the closest thing to dissent coming from linguist Mark Liberman, who writes that "fortuitous" may be undergoing a slow change leading to meaning "fortunate," but it's not there yet.

So it's fortunate for us that we can get a clear answer on this one, but it's hardly fortuitous.

I'm <u>anxious</u> to get started.

This usage is: Defensible but not advised.

*A*re you eager to learn the right way to use "anxious"? Then you should probably be anxious to learn about "eager."

That's because this usage, like so many others, gets a lot of change-o-phobes in a wad.

"My mother taught me that one *eagerly* awaits a good thing and one *anxiously* awaits a bad thing," notes a column reader named Richard.

In other words, "eager" connotes happy anticipation or excitement. "Anxious," on the other hand, has its roots in the word "anxiety," which for most of us is a lot less fun (Woody Allen fans excepted). So, "eager" good, "anxious" bad, right?

Well, yes and no. "Eager" definitely has a positive connotation. "Anxious" definitely has more of a negative connotation. But the people who would spank you for saying "I'm so anxious to get started" are a little too eager to find fault.

Take *Webster's New World College Dictionary*, for example. Yes, its first two definitions for "anxious" refer to having, experiencing, or causing anxiety. But here's *Webster's* No. 3: "eagerly wishing."

And for those who like to whine that the language has gone to pot since Richard's mama's day, you can always quote *Fowler's Modern English Usage*, which tells us that this use of "anxious" to mean "eager" dates all the way back to the eighteenth century. (So for this complaint to hold water, Richard's mama would have to be quite old indeed.) *Fowler's* tells us that's when "the adjective began to turn on its axis and came also to mean 'full of desire and endeavor; earnestly desirous.'"

Garner's Modern American Usage agrees, but at the same time issues the following advice: "When no sense of uneasiness is attached, *anxious* isn't the best word."

Usage and Abusage supports a looser definition of "anxious." *The Careful Writer* and *The Chicago Manual of Style* support the stricter one.

So can you defend using "anxious" as a synonym for "eager"? Yes. But when it counts, you should be eager to pick the best word possible to convey exactly what you want to say. In these cases, "eager" is a better bet.

78

It was <u>one of the only</u> times
a person responded to his e-mail.

This usage is: Awkward but acceptable.

*O*nly the lonely write to me about "only." And I look at all the "only" people and say: It could be worse. You could be sitting in a Starbucks thinking yourself clever for swapping out "only" with "lonely" in not one but two pop songs. (If only that weren't autobiographical.)

"I have heard what I consider to be one of the most stupid phrases in existence: *one of the only*," writes a misinformed reader named John. "I have heard this term on TV news, documentaries, and network talk shows. I have seen it in print. It infuriates me every time I see or hear it."

The people who take issue with the expression "one of the only" argue that it's illogical because "only" implies something singular: An only child. His only hope. The only person who will return his e-mails.

Therefore, they say, "one of the only" makes as much sense as "one of the one" or "one of the single."

Solid logic but built on a faulty premise. Yes, "only" usually modifies single things, but not always. In fact, two of the three definitions for this adjective in *Webster's New World College Dictionary* make it clear that "only" can also apply to plural things. Think of "The only people who showed up . . ." or "The only times I get lonely. . . ." Here we see that plural things like "people" and "times" can indeed be modified by "only."

Of course, the savviest opponents of "one of the only" say you should opt instead for "one of the few." And that's a tough point to argue.

"One of the few" seems clearer and more logical. So this is one of the few times in which you might want to cave in to the grammar snobs.

79

Eat a <u>healthy</u> diet or you could become <u>nauseous</u> and have to seek medical attention in a less <u>peaceful</u> country.

These usages are: Bitterly disputed.

Sometimes I wish all the authors in my grammar reference library were alive, a little drunk, and sitting in my living room. I'd shout out stuff like "*Chicago* says it's totally okay to use 'healthy' to mean 'healthful.' How do you like them apples, Fiskey?" Or, "Yo, Partridge. Fowler says 'peaceful' can be used to mean 'peaceable.' So stick that in your pear tree."

Then I'd just sit back and watch the fireworks—hair-pulling, wimp-slapping, fingernail-gouging, bifocals-flying-through-the-air fun.

These three word combos—healthy/healthful, nauseous/nauseated, and peaceful/peaceable—cause a ridiculous amount of trouble.

Take this reader of my column named Steve: "Being a language purist, I refuse to accept the 'modern' meanings of *nauseous* and *unhealthy*, no matter how many people interchange the words with, respectively, *nauseated* and *unhealthful*."

Or consider this from a reader named Jo: "I'm afraid the battle is lost to the use of *healthy* where *healthful* used to be correct. But it still drives me crazy to see *healthy diet*, etc."

Like these readers, there are conservative grammarians who say that there are distinctions within these pairs that are worth preserving. But at the same time, there are a lot of liberal grammarians who say that there's plenty of overlap in definitions of these words and that you can use them as they come naturally.

You can pick whichever camp you like. Just be aware that you can't hold it against someone else just for picking the opposing camp:

> "Healthy"—The conservative position is that this word means "in good health." For "promoting good health," they say use "healthful." Language liberals say it's fine to replace "a healthful diet" with "a healthy diet."

> "Nauseous"—Traditionalists insist this word means "sickening," not "sick." If you don't feel well, they say you're "nauseated." Other authorities say there's nothing wrong with saying "I feel nauseous."

> "Peaceful"—The stricter camp says this word means "serene" and usually describes locations—"a peaceful setting." For "nonwarlike," they say use "peaceable." But (you guessed it) there are at least as many respected authorities who say that this "rule" is archaic. A "peaceable country," they say, can just as rightly be described as a "peaceful country."

That's why you can get nauseous if certain people who are less than peaceful tell you to choose a diet of words that is less than healthy.

80

K-Fed is the <u>penultimate</u> rapper!

This usage is: So wrong.

There are people in the world who buy K-Fed albums. So, using this as an important lesson about taste, you would think that there would be some authorities that defend the use of "penultimate" to mean—as it's sometimes misused—"ultimate," "super-ultimate," "totally ultimate," or "K-Fedesque in its ultimateness."

But these uses are, the bosses say, just wrong. And if you use "penultimate" wrong, you'll learn all too quickly how certain people feel about it.

"I have a friend who used to use the word *penultimate* all the time, to mean *best*," writes a user named Austin at a website called WordFreaks. "It made me crazy, and I didn't want to correct him in front of other people, and so he did it in front of me for years until I couldn't take it and shouted, 'THAT WORD DOES NOT MEAN WHAT YOU THINK IT MEANS!' It kinda hurt, but he quit using it."

"Penultimate" means "second to last." As in "Jason Allen Alexander was Britney Spears's penultimate husband." (Note: While this was the case when this book went to press, in the few months it takes it to hit the shelves, her penultimate husband could be K-Fed, Tommy Lee, Larry King, or, let's face it, just about anyone.)

Not my *Webster's*, not *The American Heritage Dictionary*, not even *Merriam-Webster's* allow the use of "penultimate" as meaning "ultimate" or a revved-up version thereof. They all say it means just "second to last." The style guides that weigh in on the subject agree, making *Fowler's* citation from a 1988 *Chicago Sun-Times* piece as entertaining today as it was then:

> *Clerk:* "These are the penultimate in quality scarves!"
> *Customer:* "Well, then, show me the better line."

That's <u>a whole nuther</u> issue.

This usage is: Just please don't, okay?

*P*lease don't use "a whole nuther" or "a whole nother."

Consider "a whole other issue," "another issue entirely," "a totally different issue," "a hole udder issue"—anything but "a whole nuther."

I thank you and all the little nerve endings in my spine thank you.

This lane is for ten items or <u>less</u>.

This usage is: Apparently a linguistic crime of such magnitude that it causes more rage than LA traffic and Simon Cowell combined.

*I*n *Grammar Snobs Are Great Big Meanies,* I devoted a whole chapter to "less" versus "fewer." I went on and on about express lanes (of course) and how certain grammar snobs blow steam out their ears at signs that say "ten items or less." I even went on to explain how many of these same hotheads usually don't fully understand the difference between "less" and "fewer." They understand just enough to know that "ten items or less" is wrong but not enough to understand why "I have *one fewer* item than you" should be "I have *one less* item."

So I didn't want to get into it in this book. Been there. Done that. Spanked them.

But then, for this book, I started researching people's grammar peeves—scouring the Internet with search terms like "grammar and peeve and idiots"; searching my saved e-mails for "annoying," "infuriating," and "want to gouge my ears out with an ice pick."

And though I discovered many diverse language peeves, one kept cropping up over and over and over:

The misuse of *fewer* vs. *less* makes me grind my teeth.
—*Lisa, posting at Happy Furry Puppy Story Time*

Peeve du jour. . . . This one is getting more common, and it tweaks me mightily. *Less* versus *fewer.*
—*Trixtah, at the Random Raves portion of a personal blog site*

Alright [*sic*], my pet peeve is the confusion behind the use of the words *less* and *fewer.*
—*Bob, posting at PainInTheEnglish.com*

Bob explains his somewhat confused position: "My thought is *fewer* relates to units while *less* relates to a quality or state of being. Basically, if you can count them, use the word *fewer* and if you can't, it's *less.*"

Bob's formula will work just fine nine out of ten times, but it'll let you down hard when you must choose between "one less item" and "one fewer item."

Here's your best guideline, paraphrased from *Garner's Modern American Usage*: Use "fewer" for plural things. Use "less" for singular things.

That way, it's clear that, yes, the express lane sign should read "ten items or fewer," but you also get it right when you take a single item out of your cart and end up with "one less item."

And please, spread the word. I really, really don't want to have to go into this again in the next book (especially since that book will either be about my dysfunctional family or a number one best seller about a girl superhero named April who fights crime with her sidekick kitten Bitor at her side).

PART VIII

Conjunction-itis

83

Tell me whether <u>or not</u> you'll attend.

This usage is: Fatty.

A lot of people frown on our little "or not" in cases like this. They're the nice ones. Others hiss, spit, and hurl insults casting doubt upon whether "or not" your mama should have ever had children.

One of my readers, Melanie, had this to say on certain uses of "whether or not": "Make it stop! Please, make it stop!"

Unfortunately, this usage is so rooted in common speech that those of us used to saying it find it almost impossible to police ourselves. Still, it's good to understand the snobs' objection. And luckily, it's a simple one.

As you'll see in the next chapter, some "or nots" work great with "whether." But in uses like "Tell me whether or not you'll attend," the "or not" is "redundant," according to our friend Melanie; "superfluous," according to Garner; "a space waster," according to Fowler; and "sloppy thinking," according to Wallraff.

A good rule: If you can drop the "or not" without dropping the meaning of your sentence, it's probably a good idea to do so.

Bear in mind that this isn't exactly cut-and-dried. For example, Wallraff is willing to forgive certain users of the fatty "or not"—especially if their last name is Wallraff. "Why did you recently start a paragraph in 'Word Court' with the redundant *or not*?" one of Wallraff's readers asked. Her answer: "Just plain *whether* seems so abrupt in places. And the sentence you are writing about ('Whether or not you should use the word depends on your audience') is one such place."

The snobs will nitpick whether <u>or not</u> it does any good.

This usage is: Correct, and quite different from the last chapter's "whether or not."

I know, I know. Just when it seems you could douse every "or not" with red ink, you learn that sometimes it is needed. But this isn't as messy as it seems.

The distinction is simple. The "or not" is needed when you're emphasizing two distinct choices. Bernstein gives this example: "The game will be played whether or not it is fair." Imagine that sentence without the "or not" and you'll see why sometimes "or not" is your friend.

Another way to look at it: If you can swap out "whether" for "if," you don't need the "or not." But when that swap would change or mess up the meaning of your sentence, the "or not" is needed.

**<u>Since</u> you're reading this book,
I might as well clear up this myth, too.**

This usage is: Fine.

Some people think you can't use "since" to mean "because." They say that "since you're reading this book" is wrong because "since" refers only to a time period and not to the cause of something. In other words, they say, it's "*since* Tuesday" but "*because* you are reading this book."

I myself bought into this lore at one time and even helped spread the myth, changing every "since" in some poor reporter's article to "because." But I was a victim of a misunderstanding.

"Some writers erroneously believe that the word [since] relates exclusively to time," *The Chicago Manual of Style* says. "But the casual *since* was a part of the English language before Chaucer wrote in the fourteenth century, and it is useful as a slightly milder way of expressing causation than *because*." My other sources, including *Webster's*, agree.

So since it's best not to spread bad advice, don't take it too seriously the next time someone tells you exactly how not to use "since."

The <u>reason is because</u> I'm dense.

This usage is: Infuriating, because I keep using it, even though it's wrong.

*P*eople often ask me, "June, how'd you learn so much about grammar?" (Note, like all sentences that begin with "people often ask me," this is a lie. A more honest approach would be "Imaginary people often ask me . . ." or "In my daydreams, people ask me . . ." or, even more honestly, "In my daydreams, Brad Pitt sometimes rolls over and asks me. . . ." But writing that would mean a longer, clunkier, and less dramatic introduction that I, for one, will have no part of.) And these people go on: "Did you have a good teacher in school? Did you grow up in a house with a lot of books where the language was loved by all? Did you have an affair with William Safire?" To which I answer, "No," "No," and "No comment."

The suburban central Florida community where I went to school, I've been told, could at one time lay claim to having the highest number of trailer parks per capita nationwide. (Notice that I said "trailer parks" and not "Harvard graduates.")

The house I grew up in had more flying cockroaches than books. (It's partly a Florida thing. Try not to judge me too harshly.)

And William Safire, while hot, may or may not have been receptive to my advances. I'm not saying. And anything Billy tells you is a dirty lie.

So how, then, you are wondering, did I learn all this stuff about grammar? I learned it the hard way. By making mistakes. Many of them public mistakes, like the time I wrote "the reason is because" in a grammar column.

If a reader hadn't busted me, I'd still be writing "The reason is because . . ." at every opportunity. In fact, I still catch myself using it all the time. The reason is because I'm a hopeless case. But you don't have to be.

Here's what you do: Whenever you're tempted to write "The reason is because . . ." try swapping out "because" with "that."

The reason, experts agree, is that the "because" makes the statement redundant: As *The Careful Writer* explains, "Since the meaning of *because* is *for the reason that*, the construction is a redundancy."

H. W. Fowler said so in the 1920s. Bryan Garner renews Fowler's mandate for the twenty-first century. And others agree.

So saying "the reason is because" is kind of like saying "The explanation can be explained as . . ." or "The purpose is to serve the purpose of. . . ." It's just not necessary and it gives certain people (you know the type) cause to clobber you.

"*The reason is because* is a notorious little waste of words, no purpose being served by using both *reason* and *because* to explain oneself," Wallraff writes. "It's not so much a colloquialism as an oversight. The reason people so often say this is that they don't think back to what they've already said. Or perhaps they say it because they don't think ahead?"

"*The reason is because* . . . I'll admit makes me dig my nails into my palms," wrote essayist David Foster Wallace.

So, take it from me: Shy away from this usage. Because there's no reason to use it.

PART IX

Figures of Screech

87

Her husband <u>went missing</u>.

This usage is: Grammatical, yet despised.

*I*f grammar snobs have a maxim, it is this: Hate first, ask questions never.

That's the only possible explanation for some of the rants I've come across about the expression "went missing."

"*Went missing* must go!" writes columnist James Kilpatrick.

Oddly, he defends "went missing" on one hand by saying, "Nothing in the rules of English composition requires that idioms be plausible—or even grammatical." Nonetheless, Kilpatrick ultimately bans "went missing" because "The idiom has worn out its novelty."

There's just one problem with Kilpatrick's reasoning. "Went missing" is less an idiom than a perfectly grammatical construction.

"Went," of course, is the past tense of "go." And "go" is a very, very versatile word. Among its many definitions is "to pass into a certain condition, state, etc.; become; turn [to go mad]."

So, you could say of someone:

He went cuckoo.
He went astray.
He went native.

or

His sense of fairness and reason went missing.

"Missing" works fine as a state or condition into which you can pass. You can be missing, so you can go missing. Thus there's nothing wrong with "went missing."

This is further backed up by the fact that practically none of my reference books, not even *Fowler's* or *Garner's,* has an entry for this expression. The only authority that bothers to bring it up is *Dictionary of Disagreeable English* author Fiske, who finds it disagreeable (naturally).

88

That Principal Skinner is pure <u>milktoast</u>.

> *This usage is:* Wrong (and likely to get you ridiculed by everyone younger than Mr. Burns).

*S*ince the producers of *The Simpsons* are not yet beating down my door to beg me to write for them, I'm forced to showcase my talents here, adeptly working into this grammar book some dialogue from my hilarious *Simpsons* spec script:

> *Burns:* That Principal Skinner is pure milquetoast.
> *Homer:* Mmmm . . . milktoast.

Notice my keen sense of Homeric dialogue? Notice my brilliant contrasting of two distinct spellings that demonstrate Groening-esque insight into our two characters? Notice the web address on the back of this book through which a *Simpsons* producer might reach me to offer a job?

While I'm waiting for that sure thing to come through, I'll point out a few things about the words "milktoast" and "milquetoast."

First: The term is practically dead. Only ancient people like Mr. Burns use it or even remember where it's from. Which leads us to our second point: It's from an early-twentieth-century comic strip called *The Timid Soul,* which featured a character named Caspar Milquetoast, according to *Webster's.* Apparently, this Milquetoast person became a poster boy for passivity, with his

name coming to mean "a weak, timid person who is easily led."
That's true even though he was probably named after a delightful
dish composed of milk and toast. And that leads us to a third and
final note: To be precise, it should be spelled with a "que" and
not a "k."

A Google search produces 64,200 hits for "milktoast," suggesting it may someday close in on the 338,000 hits for "milquetoast."
But until the balance tilts some more, use "milquetoast."

Or better yet, if you're under 104 years old, just use "wuss"
instead.

89

He was hoist with his own <u>petard</u>.

This usage is: **Who cares?**

)t must have been close to deadline. Or perhaps I was sleepy or lazy or judgment-impaired from watching too much YouTube (curse your addictive ongoing saga, LonelyGirl15!). But for some reason, at one point I noticed an entry for "hoist with his own petar(d)" in *Garner's Modern American Usage* and thought, "Hey, that'll make a riveting and invaluable column for all my petar(d)-hoisting readers!"

No doubt losing fans with every word, I shared Garner's knowledge of "hoist with his own petar(d)." A petar(d), I explained, was an ancient explosive device used in battle to level gates and walls. The expression, I explained, means "to be undone by one's own scheming" and comes from *Hamlet*.

Then I got into the meat of the matter—that little "d" in the parentheses. The original *Hamlet* line, Garner explained, uses "petar." No "d."

"In modern journalistic sources, *petard* outnumbers *petar* by a 66-to-1 margin," Garner writes. "So almost every writer who uses the phrase updates Shakespeare by using *petard*."

Underscoring Garner's point, I added: "And the topper: My spell-checker doesn't recognize the word *petar*. It suggests I use *petard*."

I filed my story and went to bed, where visions of YouTube fame for my own cats danced in my head. But it didn't end there. You see, whoever edited the story at a local newspaper didn't take note of what I said about spell-checker. So when the story came out, it said, "In modern journalistic sources, *petard* outnumbers *petard* by a 66-to-1 margin." What's more, it said, "My spell-checker doesn't recognize the word *petard*. It suggests I use *petard*."

In other words, the editor's computer changed every "petar" into "petard," rendering what could have been a merely irrelevant column into something completely nonsensical.

Two nice readers—a majority of the ones I had left—sent me e-mails to let me know that something had gone wrong in the editing process. So I wrote a follow-up column, explaining why the previous week's entry appeared to be comparing identical words. I restated Garner's observation that "petard" evolved as a perversion of the *Hamlet* spelling of "petar."

The editors managed to get that one through okay. And for all that effort, I was rewarded with the following e-mail: "Every dictionary entry I have ever seen correctly spells the Medieval explosive device, the recoil force of which could hoist its operator, as p-e-t-a-r-d. Your column makes no sense, and a correction is in order.—Ken"

So now, as someone who knows how it feels to be hoisted but hard, I can honestly say that discussing, using, or caring about this archaic figure of speech is just plain petarded.

90

Bob is <u>chomping</u> at the bit to get that promotion.

This usage is: Horsefeathers.

*I*n the hit TV show *The Office,* receptionist Pam has a candy dish on her desk (and a tragic adorableness in her smile—but I digress). Though the show normally does a top-notch job of portraying real-life office dysfunction, the candy dish is the fatal flaw in an otherwise perfect depiction.

You see, I have experienced a real office candy dish firsthand. Thus, I have been to the very bowels of office hell. And I can tell you that this beloved show is glossing over some very, very ugly truths.

In a company that shall not be named, my desk was right next to the community candy supply. But at this office, the candy dish was nothing like the modest little afterthought at Pam's workstation. No, at this company "candy dish" meant a one-gallon plastic mayonnaise jar that employees took turns filling to the brim with M&Ms. And when I tell you it was an evil presence in that company, I mean a force worse than Michael Scott's racial insensitivity and Dwight Schrute's hairstyle combined. All day long, people would walk up to the jar, scoop themselves handfuls of M&Ms, and dump all their guilt right into my lap:

"I shouldn't be doing this."
"This is so bad."

"Yeah, I'm back again" (giggle).

"I had a light lunch."

"I had a light breakfast."

"I'm having a light dinner."

"I'll switch to light beer."

"That last handful was really small."

"Looks like I'll be spending an extra fifteen minutes on the treadmill tonight."

"I'm bad, bad, bad and need to be spanked by a stern mommy figure wearing a green M&M costume."

At first I was supportive: "Oh, just enjoy them." But after the ten thousandth time someone dealt with a binge by purging their shame onto my head, I cashed in my gentle language: "Hey, did you read that article about the new study proving that chocolate is less fattening if consumed within minutes of unloading your guilt on some poor coworker? You must have seen that, huh, lard butt?"

In other words, while my coworkers were *chomping* the M&Ms, I was *champing* at the bit to find some way out of my role as shame receptacle. In other words, I was *champing at the bit* to move the desk to any other spot up to and including the men's room.

"Champing at the bit" is sometimes incorrectly written as "chomping at the bit." But remember that this expression comes from horse lingo. So if you want the respect of great horsemen/linguists like John Wayne and Tonto, stick with "champing." And if you want a harmonious workplace and the admiration and respect of your colleagues, take that office candy dish and chuck it out the window.

91

For <u>all intensive purposes</u>, blogs are great sources of information.

This usage is: Wrong.

*A*s I said, researching this book has required me to spend a lot of time reading blogs—valuable time I could have spent reading the ingredients on my cereal box or biting the inside of my cheek till it bleeds. And, as I've discovered, there are a lot of blogs out there. There are the "My political party is always right and therefore I'm absolved of the burden of thinking for myself" blogs. There are the "I just finished watching *General Hospital* and now I need to commiserate with more imaginary friends" blogs. And of course there are the "My boyfriend just honked the car horn when he pulled up instead of coming to the door. Don't you think he should treat me better?" blogs.

But perhaps the most baffling of all is the "truth by committee" blog. In this method, someone posts a question—not a subjective one like "Do you think Sawyer is the hottest guy on *Lost*?" but an objective one like "What happens when you mix bleach and ammonia?". Then everyone just chimes in:

"Uh, I'm pretty sure nothing happens."

"Actually, it's a flea dip for puppies and kittens."

"No, if I remember my eighth-grade home ec, that's how you make a blancmange."

These blogs can cover any of a million different topics, but they all have one thing in common: No matter how many hundreds of armchair experts weigh in, no matter how many pages of self-congratulatory pontificating follow, not one person ever bothers to actually look anything up.

This is the blog method of choice for grammar rants, such as one I came across on the subject of "all intents and purposes" versus "all intensive purposes."

"We just had a huge disagreement about this phrase in the office," wrote the author of the Nothing But Bonfires blog. "I insisted that it was *for all intents and purposes*, while co-worker Andrew claimed that no, it was *for all intensive purposes*. Nice Canadian Damian, however, admitted that he's always said *for all intense purposes*. I think you will agree that I am OBVIOUSLY RIGHT. Right?"

Twenty-seven replies followed. Twenty-seven—all with very strong opinions on the subject (consensus: "all intents and purposes") but not one—not a single one—citing a source or even attempting to find one.

Of course, no one ever tells us where to turn for this kind of information. You can stay in college till you're forty-five and never learn of any such resource. But bloggers and message board posters take the same approach with much more easily researched stuff, like when punctuation goes inside quotation marks or how to spell "feminazi."

Plus, is it so unrealistic to hope at least one person might try a Google search? Or are the G and L keys too far away from the ones they're using to spell "I'm right"?

Luckily, you and I know by now that there are some good places to turn to for this kind of information. You can probably even guess which book I'm about to cite.

The correct expression, according to *Garner's Modern American Usage*, is "for all intents and purposes," with a note that "*to* all intents and purposes" is also acceptable, especially in Great

Britain. The wording, "all intensive purposes," Garner labels a "mondegreen"—a misheard expression.

Of all the books in my library, only two others contain entries for this expression, and both their authors—Barbara Wallraff and Robert Hartwell Fiske—agree.

So are blogs, for all intents and purposes, useless when you need accurate, reliable information? I'll look that up for you just as soon as I'm finished eating this delicious-looking blancmange.

He's at her <u>beck and</u> call.

This usage is: Right (yes, really).

I know what some of you are thinking: "What next? 'He's at her Moby and holler'? At her 'Diddy and shout'? Wouldn't '*beckon*' make a lot more sense than '*beck and*?'"

Yeah, it would, if it weren't for the fact that "beck" is a word, even without two turntables and a microphone.

A beck is "a gesture of the hand, head, etc., meant to summon," according to *Webster's New World College Dictionary*.

Garner's puts it in perspective. "*Beckon call* is an understandable guess at the phrase, since one would naturally call out to beckon someone. . . . But *beck and call* is the historical and still the greatly predominant phrase."

And that's where it's at.

It <u>remains to be seen</u> whether people will ever get their priorities straight.

This usage is: Really, who cares?

*I*n an age of terrorism, wars, global epidemics, genocide, and natural disasters up to and including *Dancing With the Stars*, columnist James Kilpatrick is upset. So upset, in fact, that he's stockpiling evidence of atrocities. Indeed, he has amassed enough newspaper clippings documenting a certain travesty of justice that he has filled a whole drawer with them.

And, based largely on this incontrovertible evidence of widespread horror, Kilpatrick is deeply, deeply disturbed. No, it's not a war or a tsunami or the sight of Jerry Springer doing the tango with a half-naked twenty-year-old that has Kilpatrick so outraged. It's something he seems to perceive as far, far worse.

I'm speaking, of course, of the shocking, disturbing, unconscionable, widespread use of "it remains to be seen."

As far back as 2003, Kilpatrick had amassed enough examples of this heinous expression to fill a whole column plus a whole desk drawer.

The *New York Times*, the *Washington Post*, *Newsweek*, the *Washington Times*, *USA Today*, *National Geographic*, and the *National Law Journal* are all guilty, Kilpatrick reported. In fact, he found so many examples of this crime against goodness and decency that he had to give "remains to be seen" the nickname "RTBS" in order to squeeze in as many as possible.

"To say that something—anything—*remains to be seen* is to make the most inane, the most banal, the most stupid observation in the annals of prophecy," Kilpatrick wrote. "Eventually, it must occur to the most thick-witted writer that every future event under moon or sun, from this nanosecond onward, *remains to be seen!*"

In other words, why would we listen to the "thick-witted writers" and editors of the most respected publications in the country when we can just put our trust in a guy who sits around nicknaming his grammar peeves (and God only knows what else)?

Surely, an abomination of this scale must also evoke the ire of Kilpatrick's colleagues in the language biz.

So let's see what Garner has to say about "RTBS." Hmmm. Nothing. That's odd. Let's check Barbara Wallraff's nationally best-selling *Word Court*. Well, this is odd indeed. Zip. How about *Fowler's*? Zilch. Bernstein? Nada. Walsh? Rien. Cranky, curmudgeonly Fiske? Niente. *AP, Chicago*, Strunk and White? Bubkes.

All this leaves us with just one question: Can someone go on living knowing he's the only person alive smart enough to get why RTBS is so "stupid"? That remains to be seen.

The baby ran down the beach <u>butt</u> naked.

This usage is: So very wrong.

I'd rather not say too much about this one. It brings back some painful memories involving a beach, a pair of training pants, and an impressionable mind overly influenced by a Coppertone billboard.

So let's just get straight to it: The term is "buck naked." "Buck," as in the hide of a deer. Not "butt," as in the body part so many people saw that tragic day in the early 1970s.

And that's all I have to say about that.

She was <u>like</u>, "Hello?!?" So he <u>goes</u>, "Whatever!"

These usages are: Slang-a-licious.

O f course these aren't proper grammar. Of course they're youthspeak. But is it really worth, like, having a cow over? Anyone? Bueller? Bueller?

Wallraff? "I see no harm in it if kids use the current kid dialect when talking with other kids, or even in casual conversation with you, as long as they can also demonstrate a command of standard English when, say, lunching with Grandmother."

Good answer, Ms. Wallraff. Now let's move on.

Happy holidays from the Smith's.

This usage is: Pretty bad, especially if you're Smith.

*I*f you ever get a card that says, "Happy Holidays from the Smith's," be afraid. Be very afraid. Because the card is raising some issues that it fails to address. For example, why does Smith refer to himself with a royal "the"? And, more important, happy holidays from the Smith's *what*?

Yes, plurals and possessives can get pretty confusing. And anyone with a last name ending in "s" has a tougher job than the rest of us.

For example, say you're a Jones. That means your whole family are the Joneses, and the house owned by all of you is the Joneses' house. Unfortunately, to your mind's eye, "the Jone's house" and "the Joneses's house" might also appear to be viable options because we've all seen similar stuff in print. (They're not options. We'll get to that in a minute.) So clearly, you Joneses have to sidestep a few pitfalls.

But Smith doesn't have the same excuse.

If you are a Smith, your family is the Smiths. If you don't have a family, yes, your house is indeed Smith's house. But it's not *the* Smith's house. And if it's owned by more than one Smith—that is, by the Smiths—you just put an apostrophe after that plural to get "the Smiths' house."

Therefore, when the Smiths wish their friends happy holidays, that wish is "from the Smiths." Plural. No possession. No apostrophe.

Simple stuff, if only you stop to think about it, which you Smiths should vow to do from now on.

Smiths dismissed.

Stevenses and Thomases and Joneses don't have it quite so easy.

For one thing, style guides add to the confusion because they disagree on how to make possessives out of proper names ending in "s." *AP* says that it's Mr. Jones' house. *Chicago* says that it's Mr. Jones's house. So even when we're just dealing with individual people, confusion is already in the cards. But note that these cases deal only with a singular. Not a plural.

When you're dealing with plurals—multiple Joneses—there's no such difference of opinion: When showing ownership by things in the plural (setting aside irregulars), you just add an apostrophe but no "s."

A yard belonging to multiple dogs is the dogs' yard. It's never the "dogs's" yard because we don't use that extra "s" when making possessives out of plurals, even though we might when making possessives out of singular words that end in "s."

A few more:

> The teachers' responsibility
> The voters' message
> The workers' meeting

And that's why it's always "the Joneses' house" and never "the Joneses's house."

Of course, if you know a guy who insists on being called The Jone, this chapter doesn't apply to him—except in letting him know he has a soul mate in that guy who calls himself The Smith.

PART X

Lingo

(The Words of Cops, Techs, and Ad Execs)

97

A store selling CDs had a sign, "SALE ON <u>CD'S</u>."

This usage is: Fine, says I.

*E*ats, *Shoots & Leaves* is a book about one woman's lifetime of traumatizing encounters with misplaced apostrophes (and other punctuation gaffes) and her long, heroic struggle to overcome them. Readers worldwide gasped and wept to read about author Lynne Truss's harrowing brushes with grocer signs reading "potatoe's and carrot's" and even more terrifying billboards for a movie then tormenting the English-speaking world, *Two Weeks Notice.* (And you thought nothing could compound the horror of a film starring Hugh Grant.)

And readers cheered Truss's courageous rallying cry as she called on the masses to mobilize, Magic Markers in hand, and brazenly ink corrections on poorly punctuated billboards and signs.

Far be it from me to deprecate her torment and triumph, but I can't help but notice a flaw in her plan for a Magic Marker militia: Many of the very people so up in arms about misused apostrophes don't know how to use them themselves. In fact, not even the rule makers can get their acts together well enough to lay down clear and widely agreed-upon guidelines.

Yes, apostrophes make possessives: "Lynne's courageous struggle." Yes, apostrophes make contractions: "Let's vandalize signs."

But there are other, not as well publicized uses for the apostrophe, summed up here by the authors of *Fowler's:* The apostrophe "is normally used in contexts where its omission might possibly lead to confusion, e.g., 'dot your i's and cross your t's'; there are three i's in inimical.'"

Does that leave a lot of room for interpretation and thus confusion? Yup. But logic will lead you down a safe path.

If you want to write about "a store selling CDs," ask yourself, is CD possessive? Is it a contraction? Clearly not. It's just a plural. So then ask, is an apostrophe needed to avoid confusion here? The answer, I'd say, is no. CDs is perfectly clear.

But if you're writing a sign in all capital letters, this formula takes a backseat: "SALE ON CD'S!"

If you left out the apostrophe here, "CDs" would be indistinguishable from a three-letter term, CDS, pronounced "See Dee Ess." So here an apostrophe helps. And best of all, according to Fowler, that's all the justification you need.

Other sources are a little less clear on this point. Many discuss initialisms like ABCs (most say no apostrophe needed here), but they stop short of considering what happens in running text that's all capitalized. That's why I'm pushing *Fowler's*—your license to use good judgment and your defense against the ink-thirsty, marauding, marker-wielding hordes.

98

The perp is <u>a male</u>.

This usage is: Fine.

*S*ome people hate to see "male" and "female" used as nouns. They should be adjectives, these people insist. So by their logic, it's okay to write "The suspect is male," because here the word "male" is functioning as an adjective. But if you write "a male," you're using it as a noun and therefore you should be subject to having your male and/or female parts put in a vise until you promise never to do so again.

While I'll be the first to admit that police lingo can get pretty silly, it doesn't mean that "male" and "female" can't be used as nouns. They are nouns, the dictionary tells us.

More fun yet: Even if they weren't nouns, you could still use them as such. Consider:

> "Roger helps the poor."
> "Mallory cares for the sick."
> "The wealthy fear Bill."
> "The best is yet to come."
> "The big and tall alike shop here."
> "Only the lonely can play."

There's a name for these. *Oxford* calls them "nominal adjectives," and defines them as "an adjective that functions as the head of a noun phrase"—that is, adjectives that do what nouns do.

So for these reasons and more, only the ignorant would criticize someone else for using "male" and "female" as nouns.

99

You're <u>pre-approved</u> for a Gougybank Card!

This usage is: Annoying, but not necessarily wrong.

*D*ear Direct Mail Marketer: Wonderful news! You're pre-approved to stop sending me mail! Based on your past history of stuffing my mailbox with tree-killing, identity-theft-risking garbage, you've been pre-approved to leave me the !*&!#% alone!

That's right: You're pre-approved to stop offering me opportunities to consolidate my high-interest credit card debt, just as you once pre-approved yourself to send me all this junk without first checking to see whether I even had any high-interest credit card debt.

Even better, you're pre-approved to look up—at any time and in any dictionary—the word "last." When you do, you'll see that you're pre-approved to stop writing "last chance" on envelopes you've been sending me every month like clockwork for more than three years!

And, best of all, you're pre-approved to hear the ugly truth: People hate marketing speak such as "pre-approved."

Clearly, the last thing I want to do is defend purveyors of this kind of marketing blather. So I have nothing but sympathy for the people who complain about the insane proliferation of the prefix "pre," like the reader who wrote to me to call this to my attention: "I get credit card ads in the mail that tell me I'm *pre-selected* or *pre-approved*. I go to the market and find *pre-stirred yogurt* and *pre-sliced bread* and *pre-sifted flour* and *pre-sweetened tea* and *pre-ground coffee*," Steve pointed out. "I go to the clothier's and find *pre-shrunk jeans*. Why add 'pre' to everything? What is wrong with advertising 'sliced bread' or 'ground coffee'?"

Steve has a point, but I wonder whether it's worth the effort.

Yes, "pre-approved," "pre-washed," "pre-shrunk," "pre-paid," "pre-qualified," and "pre-sweetened" can be redundant. But from a usage perspective, these supposed "redundancies" are all somewhat defensible. With "pre-qualified," the bank is emphasizing that you don't have to wait until after you apply for a loan in order to find out whether you'll get it. You'll get it (or so they're saying). A "pre" before "shrunk" is supposed to suggest that you won't get any big surprises the first time you open your dryer.

So yes, this "pre" is annoying. Yes, it pounds home a point that's already pretty darn clear. But perhaps focusing on the grammar isn't the best solution. Perhaps if we all agree to stop buying what the junk-mail pushers are selling, maybe the language problem will pre-approve itself to disappear forever.

100

Log <u>on to</u> the <u>website</u> and send me an <u>e-mail</u>.

These usages are: Correct, but so are some variations.

*T*he *Associated Press Stylebook* says it's "Web site," not "web-site." Yet a search of the *Los Angeles Times* archives scored only 217 matches for "Web site" (many seem to have a lowercase W, but I can't be sure because the searches aren't case sensitive) compared with 500 hits for the one-word "website" (the search function on their website seems to stop at 500 hits, suggesting there may have been many more).

This might lead you to expect a similar result from the *New York Times* archives, but you'd be wrong. A search of the New York paper's more extensive archives got 38,833 hits for two-word versions "Web site" and "web site," but only 188 for "website" and "Website."

Search both papers for "e-mail" and "email" and you'll encounter more inconsistencies, though in this case there seems to be a strong preference for "e-mail."

If anyone doubted the democratic nature of language before the technological revolution, there's no way to deny it now. The "right" and "wrong" of usage may be proclaimed by certain authorities, but the only real authority is the people.

The AP Stylebook once insisted that "on-line" be hyphenated, but people preferred "online" and *AP* finally caved.

Yet for "website"/"Web site" and similar conundrums, the jury is still out. So no one has the authority to say one is right and the other wrong.

I can, however, tell you which way the wind seems to be blowing. The one-word "website" appears to be in the lead. *AP* disagrees, but because it already says that "webcam," "webcast," and "webmaster" take one-word, lowercase forms, can a change of their "Web site" recommendation be far away?

As I said, "e-mail" seems to be the choice of style books, even though actual users like "email" an awful lot, too.

"Internet" gets the proper-name treatment, capital "I" and all, in *AP* and *Chicago*.

And this seems as good a place as any to point out a related issue: Stick with "log on to" the Internet, not "log onto." That's because "on" is treated as part of the verb. "To log on" is a verb phrase with an entirely different meaning from "to log."

So yes, you step onto a platform, get onto a topic of conversation, or walk onto the carpet, but keep the "on" separate when it's integral to the verb's meaning, as in "log on to" and "sign on to."

101

The <u>suspect</u> robbed the bank.

This usage is: Imprecise and could even get you sued.

*I*f you're like me, you watch the local news every night with one thought outweighing all others: What could possibly be done to make this experience even more annoying?

Sure, the program could expand its car chase coverage, perhaps putting reporter Fritz Neverbalds in a fake cop car in hopes random outlaws will see it and bolt like the wind. Sure, they could get more creative with their nightly scare tactics—"There's a violent criminal trying to break into your home right now; we'll tell you what he's armed with right after sports and the weather with Smiling Cirrus McCloud." Perhaps the coanchors could just talk to each other more, offering even more astute insights on the cuteness of the previous segment's puppy. Or maybe they could just find a way to squeeze in even less real news.

But clearly, our local news people just aren't willing to go the extra mile to elevate their own annoyingness to truly preternatural levels. So it's up to us, the viewers, to look for creative ways to make the experience more unbearable.

This is a time when it actually pays to take a page from the grammar snobs' book by scrutinizing the newscasters' every word, especially when one of them is talking about a "suspect." Because when it comes to proving that a reporter's brain is in the off mode, there's no better word than "suspect."

If you pay attention, you'll probably notice something like "The suspect got more than $1,200 from the cash register, then fled on foot." But *Webster's* says a suspect is a person who is suspected of something, most notably a crime. Therefore, the suspect didn't rob the bank. The robber robbed the bank.

The language experts who weigh in on this agree—especially the ones who actually work in the news business, like Bill Walsh and Barbara Wallraff.

Oftentimes when news people use the word "suspect," there's no real suspect involved. They know *someone* robbed the bank, but they don't have the first clue who. So in those cases, referring to a criminal as a suspect is just silly.

But in cases where police have fingered a potentially guilty person, reporters' misuse of the word "suspect" can get downright libelous. For example, if you happened to be walking down the street in front of the bank wearing a ski mask and carrying a squirt gun at the exact moment the place was robbed, you could easily find yourself in custody. Then, a reporter who said, "The suspect stole more than $1,200 from the bank," would technically be saying that you stole it. That's because while you're not the perpetrator, you are the suspect. And you didn't do it.

In our great country, we're all innocent until proven guilty, whether the crime is robbing a bank or ripping the toupee off of Fritz Neverbalds. So suspects aren't necessarily criminals and that thing on Fritz's head, despite how it looks, may not be a dead prairie dog.

The Princess and the Peeveless:

An Epically Pollyanna-ish Epilogue

*A*nd so the people read the princess's important book, and learned all about the one hundred and one most-attacked sentences. And never again did they utter the incorrect usages. Nor did they shrink from using good English that once drew the ire of misguided snobs.

And above all, never, ever did the wicked wordsmiths of the Western world find other words or sentences to serve as objects of their ire. Indeed, the deposed snobs saw the error of their ways. And they harnessed their peevish powers for more worthy pursuits, such as making life difficult for SUV drivers or mocking people who can't order coffee in fewer than ten syllables.

And they all (except the SUV drivers and Starbucks soliloquists) lived happily ever after.

Acknowledgments

There are so many people without whom this book would not have been possible. So if you've got a beef, take it up with them. They are:

David Cashion, my editor, who—there's no better way to put it—rocks: In a publishing world where authors seem to constantly report pretty unpleasant experiences with editors, I landed one who makes me want to bake him cupcakes with heart-shaped sprinkles. He's good. Really good. He can take one look at a manuscript and see how it can be better. But even more amazing, he just rocks as a human being.

Laurie Abkemeier, my agent: How I scored her I'll never know. She is what aspiring authors refer to as a "dream agent"—and they don't even know her. In addition to being on top of her game, she's also professional, reliable, trustworthy, savvy, nice, genuinely adorable, and a fellow cat lover. When I'm worried about how I'm measuring up as a writer, not only is she willing to take the time to make me feel better, she actually can. Oh, yeah. And she gets me money, too.

Laura Tisdel: Laura is evidence that something funny is going on at Penguin—a mysterious dynamic keeping the place so human that it's hard to believe it's one of those big, scary publishing houses I once feared. Laura was my publicist for the last book. She has now moved on to the editorial side. And though she wasn't even assigned to work with me on *Mortal Syntax*, we became so like friends on the last one that it truly feels as if she were part of it.

Lindsay Prevette: Laura's replacement on the publicity side is professional, nice, smart, effective, and someone whose passion and ideals I deeply admire and whose company I really enjoy.

Penguin copy editors: These people bust their humps to make others look good and take none of the credit for themselves.

Stephanie Diani, Jessica Garrison, Jeannie Wallace, Bill Mikulak, Mallory King, Kimberly Dickens, Elizabeth Reday, Michael Soller, Chris Read, Pat and Ed Averi, Paul Averi, Angela Averi, Alison McCarthy, Fran and Frank Diani, John and Lourdes Brown, Roger Johnson, Melissa Ulloa, Paul Clinton, Sandy Crosier, Julie McCaskie, Nancy McCabe, Richard and Ronni Basis, and Donna Stallings: These are friends. I could go into an explanation of how their friendship helped this book, but the truth is "friends" says more than any other explanation could.

Dr. Marisa DiPietro: I'm not even going to tell you what she did (yet). She knows. But trust me, it's un-freakin'-believable.

Diane Casagrande, Jennifer Savage, and Melanie Sorli: These are my sisters. Those among them who had the opportunity to pull my hair, did. Those who had no such opportunity surely would have had I been closer or had they been bigger. That's what sisters do (as far as I can tell). They have helped make me who I am today and I love them for it.

Lisa Wood, Maitreya Friedman, Gina Fields, John Peters, Shannon McEachern, and Mike Siegel: These are the members of my writing group who inspire me, support me, make me a better writer, and with their own writing set a very high bar indeed. (When they become huge, remember you saw their names here first.)

Carolyn Howard-Johnson, Christa Faust, Treacy Colbert, Jenna Ryan, Maxine Nunes, Naomi Hirahara, Alexandra Sokoloff,

Ina Rometsch: These are the members of my Women Writers' Lunch Club who make me feel, even as I'm sitting alone in front of my computer, that I'm part of a sisterhood of cool, fun, interesting writers out there who are also sitting alone in front of computers. In other words: not so alone. Carolyn, besides being a friend, poet, and teacher, is also a book marketing expert who is so generous with her wisdom and experience that it blows my mind.

Danette Goulet and all the editors of the *Glendale News-Press, Burbank Leader, Venice Beach Gondolier*, and *Kilgore News-Herald:* for carrying my weekly column regardless of whatever their readers might say.

Most of all, there's Ted Averi: Oy. What do you say about a man who loves you, excites you, supports you, encourages you, believes in you, plus is a really good editor? The first thing that comes to mind is "Hands off, ladies." But the most important thing is "Thank you, Ted."

Thank you all.

Sources

The American Heritage Dictionary of the English Language, 4th ed. Boston: Houghton Mifflin, 2006.

The American Heritage Dictionary, Second College Edition. Boston: Houghton Mifflin, 1985.

The Associated Press Stylebook. New York: Basic Books, 2004.

Bernstein, Theodore M., *The Careful Writer: A Modern Guide to English Usage*. New York: The Free Press, 1993.

Burchfield, R. W., *Fowler's Modern English Usage*, revised 3rd ed. New York: Oxford University Press, 2004.

The Chicago Manual of Style, 15th ed. Chicago: University of Chicago Press, 2003.

Fiske, Robert Hartwell, *The Dictionary of Disagreeable English: A Curmudgeon's Compendium of Excruciatingly Correct Grammar*. Cincinnati: Writer's Digest Books, 2004.

Freeman, Jan, "The Word," *Boston Globe*, various dates 2005 to 2007.

Garner, Bryan A., *Garner's Modern American Usage*. New York: Oxford University Press, 2003.

Greenbaum, Sydney, *The Oxford English Grammar*. New York: Oxford University Press, 1996.

Kilpatrick, James J., "The Writer's Art," Universal Press Syndicate, uexpress.com, various dates 2001 to 2006.

Liberman, Mark, and Geoffrey K. Pullum, *Far from the Madding Gerund and Other Dispatches from Language Log*. Wilsonville, OR: William James & Co., 2006.

Merriam-Webster Online, merriam-webster.com.

Oxford Universal Dictionary. London: Rand McNally & Co., Conkey Division, 1955.

Partridge, Eric, *Usage and Abusage*, First American Edition. New York: Barnes & Noble Books, 1995.

Rozakis, Laurie E., *The Complete Idiot's Guide to Grammar and Style*. Indianapolis: Alpha Books, 2003.

Strunk, William Jr., and E. B. White, *The Elements of Style*, 4th ed. Boston: Allyn and Bacon, 2000.

Wallace, David Foster, *Consider the Lobster and Other Essays*. New York: Little, Brown and Co., 2006.

Wallraff, Barbara, *Word Court*. San Diego: Harcourt Inc., 2000.

Walsh, Bill, *Lapsing into a Comma: A Curmudgeon's Guide to the Many Things That Can Go Wrong in Print—and How to Avoid Them*. Chicago: Contemporary Books, 2000.

———, *The Elephants of Style: A Trunkload of Tips on the Big Issues and Gray Areas of Contemporary American English*. New York: McGraw-Hill, 2004.

Webster's New World College Dictionary, 4th ed. Cleveland: Webster's New World, 2001.